STAIRLIFT TO HEAVEN

by

Terry Ravenscroft

Published in 2011 by FeedARead Publishing

Copyright © Terry Ravenscroft, 2011

The book cover artwork is copyright to Tom Unwin

British Library C.I.P.

A CIP catalogue record for this title is available from the British Library.

About the author

The day after Terry Ravenscroft threw in his mundane factory job to become a television comedy scriptwriter he was involved in a car accident which left him unable to turn his head. Since then he has never looked back.

Before they took him away he wrote scripts for Les Dawson, The Two Ronnies, Morecambe and Wise, Alas Smith and Jones, Not the Nine O'Clock News, Ken Dodd, Roy Hudd, and several others. He also wrote the award-winning BBC radio series Star Terk Two.

Born in New Mills, Derbyshire, in 1938, he still lives there with his wife Delma and his mistress Divine Bottom (in his dreams).

email terryrazz@gmail.com
facebook http://on.fb.me/ukZ78e
twitter http://bit.ly/t0mVyB
website www.topcomedy.co.uk
blog www.stairlifttoheaven.com

Also by Terry Ravenscroft

CAPTAIN'S DAY
JAMES BLOND - STOCKPORT IS TOO MUCH
INFLATABLE HUGH
FOOTBALL CRAZY
DEAR AIR 2000
DEAR COCA-COLA
LES DAWSON'S CISSIE AND ADA
I'M IN HEAVEN
THE RAZZAMATAZZ FUN EBOOK
ZEPHYR ZODIAC
CALL ME A TAXI
GOOD OLD GEORGE!
STAIRLIFT TO HEAVEN 2 - FURTHER UP THE
STAIRLIFT
IT'S NOT CRICKET!

STAIRLIFT TO HEAVEN

FOREWORD

The day before my sixty-fifth birthday I decided to start a journal that would chronicle the first five years of my life as an old age pensioner. The journal would largely be about my being old, about what it's like to be an old age pensioner - I don't like the term 'Senior Citizen', people my age are old and we draw a pension, neither is anything to be ashamed of, so why call ourselves senior citizens? Senior to whom? Try going to the chip shop and telling the yobbo with the number one haircut and the number four brain that you're senior to him and therefore entitled to go before him in the queue and you'll soon find out whether you're a senior citizen or not.

My intention was not to write something every day, as with a diary, but only to record events that might be of interest. Therefore there are large time gaps in the narrative; if nothing interesting happened to me for a month then I didn't write anything. There are quite enough uninteresting things being published nowadays without my adding to the total.

Given my background and what people have come to expect from me I have confined myself largely to events of a humorous nature: however I have also included a few 'more serious' items that I feel might be of use to people of a similar age as me, in the hope that the benefit of my experiences may be of help to them in their pensioner years.

Whilst all the events in the journal are true the dialogue is not a hundred per cent accurate, but as I remembered it.

However it is always true in spirit and if I am guilty of embellishing it here and there it is only to make for a more entertaining read. A few names and place names have been altered to protect the guilty.

I have called my journal 'Stairlift to Heaven'. It is a metaphorical stairlift on which I ride - as yet I have no need of the real thing, and sincerely hope I never will. But at my time of life I am certainly on it, sat at the bottom with St Peter and the Pearly Gates awaiting me at the top.

I cordially invite you to join me on my ride on the Stairlift to Heaven.

The principal *dramatis personae* in 'Stairlift to Heaven' are as follows.

Me. Now aged seventy-one next birthday. (I have learned that people of my age, when asked how old they are, never say the age they are at the moment but what age they will be next. Hopefully that is.) Ex-television and radio scriptwriter. Wrote for Les Dawson, The Two Ronnies, Morecambe and Wise, Not the Nine-o-clock News, Alas Smith and Jones and a few others. Wrote the radio series Star Terk 2. Now writes humorous novels.

My wife, Delma. Now aged sixty-eight. Hereafter always referred to as 'The Trouble'. I call her this not because of the cockney rhyming slang thing, trouble and strife, wife, but because she has a habit, when addressing me, of beginning her sentences with the words 'The trouble with you is....' Sometimes, when I have clearly upset her, she will insert my full Christian name, 'Terence' between the words 'you' and 'is'....*viz*, "The trouble with you, Terence, is...." If she stresses either 'you' or 'Terence' I batten down the hatches. You'll see.

Atkins, from down the road. Now aged seventy. Atkins is a great friend of mine, a kindred spirit. I first met him about ten years ago when the Inland Revenue called me in to explain my debatable - their expression - claims for certain expenses incurred whilst following my profession. Atkins was the official delegated to grill me. In the event little or no grilling took place as we got on like a house on fire from the moment I mentioned that I used to write scripts for Les Dawson. Atkins turned out to be being a huge fan of Les and we spent about an hour talking about him and then about two minutes talking about my expenses claim, which Atkins then accepted without question.

During the interview it transpired that not only did Atkins live in the same town as me, but on the same road, about twenty doors down. We had been living in close proximity for the past five years, completely oblivious of each other, like near neighbours often do. Ours would seem to be the most unlikely of friendships considering our previous occupations, inasmuch as I spent my working life trying to make people laugh whereas Atkins made his living trying to make them cry. However in many other ways we share similarities; we are the same age, we both have a healthy distrust of solicitors, financial advisers and politicians, and we share the same sense of humour, or, as The Trouble succinctly if rather unkindly puts it, "Atkins is as daft as you are." And although Atkins is sometimes responsible for getting me into some situations I would rather not be in, our occasional departures from sanity re-charges our batteries and makes life a little less run-of-the-mill and thus more bearable. We are neither of us are the worse for it and we like to think it keeps us young.

So here we go then:-

March 9 2006. *HAPPY BIRTHDAY.*

Today I am sixty-five. In my head I feel like I'm twenty five; in fact I've been twenty-five in my head ever since I was twenty-five everywhere else, some forty years ago. Probably in an effort to compensate for this my body is well over sixty-five, at least eighty-five I would guess judging from all the aches and pains and things wrong with it. However in my mind's eye I still look exactly the same as I did when I was twenty-five; no oil painting, but at least not the faded water colour that now looks back at me bleary-eyed from the bathroom mirror every morning.

Imagining myself to be still twenty-five catches me out sometimes, especially if I have accidentally made eye contact with someone young; for nowadays younger people, and especially young women, look straight through me. It's not that they disregard me; they don't even see me. It's as if I'm The Invisible Old Man. I could easily sit in on their conversation without fear of being noticed. However, not wishing to learn how cool are the latest inane rantings of someone called Twopence Ha'penny or some other fanciful name, or how bladdered they all got last Friday night and wasn't it funny when Melissa chucked up all over the chucker out, I have somehow managed to get by without that diversion. I suppose I was just the same when I was that age; although I remember myself as being quite perfect.

Two weeks prior to my sixty-fifth birthday I had received a letter from the local hospital, Stepping Hill (known to everyone as 'Step in ill, come out dead', not wholly without some justification). It informed me that I was to present myself at 10 a.m. on that day for a bladder examination. I showed the letter to The Trouble.

"That's a nice birthday present for you," she said, ever the droll.

"I'd rather they'd given me a pair of socks," I said.

Having now had the bladder examination I would rather have had *anything* else. A pair of socks with a tarantula in each toe would have been lovely. A pair of underpants with a scorpion in them. A pair of trousers with a man-eating tiger in one leg and Jaws in the other. Bring them on. I once had a prostate examination that involved the doctor inserting his finger up my bottom and poking it about as though he were searching for a pound coin that had fallen down the back of the settee, which I thought was pretty painful. It was nothing. Compared to the bladder examination it was the caress of a lover.

Incidentally, quite a bit of the rest of these opening pages is about my waterworks. I'm afraid this can't be avoided if I'm going to start at my sixty-fifth birthday as the first thing of note worth recording, given that The Trouble failed to give me breakfast in bed, or anything else for that matter, involves my waterworks. It won't all be about my waterworks, but a fair bit of it will. However it's doubtful I will be mentioning it again - my waterworks won't be hanging over you whilst you're reading the rest of the book, in a manner of speaking. But in the meantime you'll just have to grin and bear it. As I did with my bladder examination.

I've had trouble with my prostate gland for at least ten years, probably nearer fifteen, and I have to pass water quite frequently. About twenty times a day on average.

That's bad enough, but having found a place in which to pass water I can't pass it, usually for a couple of minutes or so, but quite often for five minutes, even longer sometimes. At first I just stood there waiting. Then, to fill in the time, I started counting how many ceramic tiles there were on the walls - in our bathroom there are a hundred and eighty four, two of them cracked, but in an old-fashioned Victorian public convenience in Manchester I once counted four hundred and twenty three before the fountain started to flow. However tile counting gets a bit boring after a while so I started dreaming up other things to do to pass the time, given that I was temporarily incapable of passing anything else. Eventually I ended up with quite a few, so now, in the interests of helping any fellow sufferers who may also be at a loose end in similar circumstances - or more accurately an unloose end - here they are.

1. Do a crossword puzzle. My first job every morning is to cut out the crossword from the Daily Telegraph and prop it on the toilet roll holder in the bathroom. On average I fill in about six answers per visit so after about seven visits I've usually finished it. A word of warning though; if you have visitors who are likely to want to use the lavatory find somewhere to keep the crossword other than propped on the toilet roll, especially if the toilet roll needs changing and there's only the cardboard tube left, as in the past I've lost a couple of half-completed crosswords that have been used as emergency toilet paper and have had to go out and buy another Daily Telegraph.

2. Do a few simple keep-fit exercises. However, on no account do any exercise which involves rotating the hips from side to side because if your waterworks suddenly decides to start up you might find yourself peeing on the bathroom floor, with all the subsequent earache from your wife that peeing on the bathroom floor inevitably brings with it.

3. Sing (daytime only). Don't be embarrassed, people sing in the bath so why not in the bathroom whilst waiting to pee? I've been doing it for years and while my peeing has been getting increasingly poorer my singing has got increasingly better, so much so that Mrs Baxter next door sometimes sends in requests. For added enjoyment give some point and focus to your singing. I once sang the first line of twenty-seven Frankie Laine songs and it would have been twenty eight if the twenty-seventh hadn't been 'Cool Clear Water', which set me off peeing.

4. Make plans for the day. On one waiting to pee occasion I planned to mow the lawn, weed the flowerbeds, wash the car, clear out the garage, put up a kitchen shelf and change a light bulb. However I only managed to change the light bulb as I spent most of the day waiting to pee.

5. Read a book. Word of warning though; be careful in your choice of literature. Over the course of four days I once read 'The Exorcist' whilst waiting to pee, but at times it got so exciting I carried on reading it after I'd had a pee and was halfway to wanting the next pee before I realized, and by then it was hardly worth while going downstairs again. So to ensure you don't spend any more time than necessary standing at the lavatory pick a book you will be glad to put down after you've finished peeing. I recommend something by Jeffrey Archer or Jilly Cooper, or anything by Tolkien.

Young boys with waterworks trouble should read Harry Potter. Adults who read Harry Potter deserve to have trouble with their waterworks and should be made to read a proper book.

6. Put a television in the bathroom and watch Daytime TV. The programmes are absolute drivel, but there is something oddly satisfying and not inappropriate about watching 'This Morning', 'Trisha' and 'Loose Women' with your dick hanging out.

But back to my bladder examination.

I hadn't really thought much about how the nurse was actually going to examine my bladder but if I'd been asked to hazard a guess I would have suggested it might be something not dissimilar to having an X-ray of the digestive system after swallowing a barium meal. I couldn't have been more wrong.

As requested I had undressed and put on the smock-like garment beloved of hospitals, the one for which you need the abilities of a contortionist to tie the strings at the back, and which, if by some miracle you have managed to tie them, need the skills of Houdini to untie them, and was now seated nonchalantly with my legs dangling over the side of the operating table awaiting the ministrations of the nurse who had been charged with carrying out the procedure. I hadn't observed anything overtly pain-inflicting amongst the apparatus laid out in antiseptic neatness on the nearby table, so it was more to make conversation than a search for knowledge that I asked the nurse what the two long thin plastic tubes were for.

"I insert them in your penis and push them down into your bladder," she said, matter of fact.

I blinked. "Down my penis?"

The nurse nodded. I gulped. "Both the tubes?"

The nurse affirmed this with another curt nod. I gulped twice, once for each tube. "At the same time?"

She nodded a third time. I didn't ask for any more details as I was sure it would only elicit another nod and I wasn't at all sure I'd be able to handle the things she'd already nodded for.

"There'll be a bit of discomfort," she added.

This snippet of information seemed to me to be about as necessary as telling someone who was about to be hung, drawn and quartered that it wasn't going to be a picnic. It crossed my mind that being hung, drawn and quartered might be preferable to the bladder examination, and I was just about to ask the nurse if this was an option when she went into action.

"Lie down please," she said, snapping on a pair of rubber gloves in the expert way that all medical staff do, probably in the hope that it demonstrates their efficiency, when all it achieves is to fill you with an even greater sense of dread.

Although the nurse wasn't particularly attractive she was still a young woman and I must confess that initially I was more than a little worried there might be some spontaneous and unwelcome stirrings in my loins once she'd started to handle my private parts. Believe me, after realising what the nurse was about to do to me she could have been as desirable as Angelina Jolie and assisted by Nurse Cameron Diaz on one side and Nurse Penelope Cruz on the other and my penis would still have remained as limp as Dale Winton's wrists.

"This will help deaden the pain," she said, spraying my genital area with an aerosol. Having done this she selected one of the pieces of plastic tubing and eyed me ominously.

I had no wish to see what she was about to do with the tube, enduring it would be bad enough, so clamped my eyes firmly shut. The nurse went about her business. It was immediately obvious that the moment I closed my eyes she had swapped the thin plastic tubing for a Dyno-Rod, for surely it was something capable of clearing blocked drains that she then started shoving down my urethra with gay abandon.

I had no way of knowing whether the anaesthetic spray helped to deaden the pain but felt that if it did it was wasting its time, for the pain was truly excruciating. When I was in the army a bloke in my platoon had been unfortunate enough to catch gonorrhoea, the symptoms of which he reported were 'Like pissing broken glass'. By the time the two plastic tubes had been pushed into my penis as far as the nurse deemed sufficient I felt like I was passing not broken glass but broken bottles, and very large bottles at that.

The tubes inserted, I then had to stand up, my smock pulled up and gathered round my waist so that it wouldn't foul the plastic pipes now dangling from my willy, whilst the nurse proceeded to slowly pump what seemed like the contents of Lake Superior into my bladder.

After about two minutes pumping she said, "Tell me when you can't take any more."

"I can't take any more," I said, almost before she'd got the words out of her mouth.

She pumped a few more times for good luck, hers, not mine, then, while I was still standing there holding the smock round my waist trying desperately to pretend I was somewhere else she consulted a graph on the machine that had been monitoring what had been going on in my bladder while she'd been pumping it full of water. After making

14

copious notes for what seemed longer than the time it took Tolstoy to write 'War and Peace' she pointed to a plastic bucket. "You can empty your bladder in there now," she said. Then, getting to her feet, she added, primly, "I'll go outside while you do it, I wouldn't want to embarrass you."

She started to make for the door. I called out. "Nurse!"

She stopped. "Yes?"

"Nurse," I said, with great patience, "I have just lain down on an operating table while you inserted two plastic tubes down my penis. I then had to stand up, still exposing everything I've got, while you pumped God knows how many gallons of water into my bladder. How could I possibly be any more embarrassed than I already am?"

She just smiled and went out. On her return she removed the plastic tubes. Immediately the pain, which had by then diminished slightly, became so bad that I almost asked her to put them in again. However faced with the prospect of walking about for the rest of my life with two tubes hanging from my John Thomas I managed to resist. A couple of hours later the pain had worn off to such an extent that it was only about as painful as hitting your thumb with a lump hammer.

I told The Trouble all about the experience when I got home. She was most concerned.

"We're still going out for a meal tonight are we? Because if not I'll have to get something out of the freezer."

"What?"

"We were going out for a meal to celebrate your birthday, remember?"

"We still are."

"You can walk all right?"

"They put the tubes down my penis, not my legs."

15

"Because the way you were going on about it I thought you'd need at least a week in bed to get over it," she said, in that sarcastic tone that women employ every time men claim they are in pain.

I didn't argue. I learned my lesson long ago. Whenever men complain of pain women always play the 'pain of childbirth' card and I wasn't having any of that nonsense.

Note: No experience is wasted in the writing game and I used the events of my bladder examination as the basis of the final chapter of my novel 'James Blond-Stockport Is Too Much'.

****

That evening, when we went to the pub, the waitress was one of those young bare-midriff jobs. I'm sure the only reason she noticed me was because noticing old people who are awaiting the attentions of a waitress is in her job description.

"Do you have any proof you're a pensioner?" she asked.

We'd been to the Red Lion a few times previously. The food there isn't bad, although largely limited to 'baked potato with' meals, but the main reason we'd chosen it above somewhere with a more ambitious menu is because it's within easy walking distance of our home, an advantage which also enables us to share a bottle of wine without fear of being breathalysed. A further encouragement is that old age pensioners and their spouses qualify for a twenty five per cent discount on Wednesdays. Before ordering I had thought it prudent to stake my claim to this right, hence the challenge from the waitress, which took me somewhat by surprise.

"Pardon?" I said, noting that about three inches of her knickers were showing above the top of her trousers, and they were inside out too unless they've started putting the label on the outside. A few years ago women took great pains not to reveal Visible Panty Line, now they don't even mind showing visible panties. I gave up trying to understand women long ago.

"Anybody could say they're a pensioner," said Bare-midriff. "I have to have proof."

My first thought was to point to my balding head of grey hair, tell her at length about my waterworks problems - including that morning's bladder examination - take out my false teeth and put them on the table and say, "How's that for starters?" However before I could The Trouble, sensing a scene, stepped in and said, "That's all right, no problem, we'll pay the full price."

"Suit yourself," said Bare-midriff.

I couldn't let that go without getting in at least one dig at the little madam. "We are not suiting ourselves," I told her, "We are suiting you and your disbelieving nature; which is just about all I have come to expect from little minxes like you with a ring through their navel."

Whether it was my little outburst that was the cause of what followed or if it was just because she was plain stupid I don't know. Probably a bit of both.

"I'll have a baked potato and beef casserole, please," said The Trouble, steadying the ship, and polite as always.

"I'll have the same," I said. Then I noticed they had a blackboard special, battered haddock and chips. "No, hold that. I'll have the battered haddock. With a baked potato, please."

"We don't do baked potato and battered haddock."

What was this? I said,"You have battered haddock, don't you?"

She nodded.

"And you have baked potatoes?"

"Yes. But not together. The battered haddock and chips is a special, we're not allowed to mess about with specials."

"I'm not asking you to mess about with it. All I'm asking you to do is to replace the chips with a baked potato."

She batted this back as effortlessly as Don Bradman in his prime facing a rookie bowler. "That's messing about with it."

I considered the problem for a moment. I was aware it wouldn't be an easy one to crack; after all I was dealing here with someone who didn't have the brains to put her knickers on the right way round, let alone see sense. Nevertheless I managed to come up with a solution. "Could you do a battered haddock and chips, and leave off the chips?"

She thought about it for a moment. "You'll have to pay for the chips."

"No problem. Could you also do me a baked potato and a beef casserole, but leave off the beef casserole?" Then, anticipating her answer, "Which I know I will have to pay for."

"Yes," she said, though now with a little uncertainly, with the air of someone who suspected she was being talked into something, but not knowing what. She was.

"Excellent." I said. "Could you then take the baked potato off its plate and put it on the plate that contains the battered haddock, then bring it to me."

Her reply was immediate and uncompromising. "That's battered haddock and baked potato."

"Yes," I smiled.

"We don't do battered haddock and baked potato."

"Come on," I said to The Trouble, getting to my feet, "We're going."

"The trouble with you is...." she started, but I was halfway to the door by then.

On the way home we got a takeaway from the Chinese down the road: sweet and sour pork, beef in black bean sauce, egg fried rice, prawn crackers. I asked the owner if I could have a discount even though I couldn't prove I was an old age pensioner. He said he wouldn't give me a discount even if I could prove I was Confucius.

Happy birthday.

****

April 27 2006. *GOODRAMGATE.*

The trip to the charity shops of York had gone off reasonably well until Harrison spoiled it by shitting in Atkins's trousers.

Atkins and I, accompanied by Harrison and Hargreaves, acquaintances of Atkins, had been moved into taking the trip to York in response to an email I'd had from John Laithwaite, an old friend of mine.

I've always felt that charity shops are a perfect example of the distribution of wealth, stocked as they are largely by donations from twenty to sixty-five-year olds, people in work, and frequented largely by people under twenty and old age pensioners, people not in work. I've always made good use of them, hence the email from my friend John, who, aware of this, let it be known that he'd recently been on a trip to York and had been greatly enthused by the abundance of charity shops to be found there. He went on to say that there must be at least forty, and of that number upwards of twenty were to be found in one of the city's main thoroughfares, Goodramgate, close to the famous Minster.

The only fly in the ointment, John warned, is that York is a university city and as such is infested with a large population of students, and that because the vast majority of students are poor the charity shops are an obvious attraction as not only do they offer them the opportunity to rig themselves out in decent clothes but do so without causing too much of a dent in their beer money. Consequently students are frequent and voracious users of the shops and this often brings about occasions when a non-student charity shopper and a student make for the same item. The way to deal with them when this happens, advises John, is to poke them sharply in the ribs with the pointed end of a rolled umbrella, or, if they are particularly persistent, an electric cattle prod.

York is a lovely city, one of my favourites, and John's email reminded me that it had been far too long since I'd last walked its impressive walls. News of all the charity shops to be found within those walls - especially in Goodramgate, which sounded to me to be very much like the Bond Street of charity shopping - only increased my desire to pay it another visit, and very soon; charity shops were certainly not there in anything like that number when I last visited York, but that must have been about ten years ago, the scale on which you get them nowadays being a quite recent phenomenon.

I mentioned John's email to Atkins, who is an even keener patron of charity shops than I am, quite unable to turn down a bargain, and, courtesy of the joint efforts of Help the Aged and Oxfam, probably the only man ever to venture out in broad daylight dressed in a bowler hat and a kilt in the tartan of the MacGregor clan. This he did when we went together to the 2002 Commonwealth Games in nearby Manchester and he wanted to see if dressed in that fashion he could get into the Lawn Bowling for free by telling the man on the gate he was the entry from British Caledonia. The man on the gate, dressed in an even more bizarre manner than Atkins in the official Games uniform of multi-coloured shell suit, flat hat and trainers, took one look at him and let him in without batting an eyelid.

The upshot was that Atkins and I decided on a trip to York in the not too distant future. This would be followed by a visit to the Jorvik Viking Centre, which neither of us had visited before, and where Atkins hoped to get in for nothing provided he could pick up a helmet with horns in it at one of the charity shops.

The day before the trip I popped into our local Age Concern; spring had suddenly arrived, I was short on lightweight trousers, and I thought if I could pick up a decent pair I'd be able to wear them on our outing.

Many people draw the line at buying clothes from charity shops on the grounds that there's a fair chance that previously they will have been worn by someone who has died, but the only way this would ever put me off buying them would be if the man who had died was still in them, and even then I still might be tempted if they were in better condition than he was. Whenever I'm considering the purchase of new trousers I always ask myself which I would rather have, a brand new pair of trousers or a pair of second-hand trousers with lots of wear left in them, plus a couple of bottles of decent wine. The second-hand trousers and wine win every time.

When I entered the shop I noticed a new assistant behind the counter. When I say 'new' I mean new to the job, as opposed to not old, it apparently being a rule in charity shops that none of the staff should be younger than ninety and have the appearance of someone who is in far more need of charity than the customers. In this instance the new assistant passed with flying colours, or maybe, given her advanced years, shuffling colours.

As is my custom with all new members of staff at Age Concern, on first making their acquaintance, I put on a worried expression, hobbled up to the counter and said, "I'm concerned about my age." This always gets one of two responses: - (a) They look at me for a few seconds as though I'm stark-raving mad and set about tidying the nearest rack of clothes, or (b), they say: "We only sell second-hand clothes and books and things." However on this occasion the new assistant rang the changes. She looked at me up and down and said, "Well we all have to go some time, love, but I'm sure you've got time to buy something before you pop off." She should do well.

In all charity shops the stock of women's clothes outnumber men's by a ratio of about seven to one. This isn't, as one might suspect, because women are seven times more generous in the gift of their cast-offs, but because they have seven times more clothes to cast off, as any man who has compared the contents of his wife's wardrobe with his own modest collection of clothing will be only too well aware. Consequentially the men's section is only one-seventh as large as the women's section and can usually be found, just, hidden away in the farthest corner of the sales floor from the door. This is the case with my local Age Concern.

There were about a hundred pairs of trousers on offer, a hundred and six if you include the five pairs of combat trousers and a pair of jodhpurs, but as it's unlikely I will ever be waging war on anyone, especially on horseback, I passed up on them. I soon found something suitable, a nice pair of Chinos in pensioner grey, and took them to the counter to be bagged and paid for. The new assistant regarded them with approval. "Very nice," she said. "They should last you a lifetime." Then she cracked a horrible smile. I shall have to watch that one.

The following day, when our party arrived in York, we discovered that the shops in Goodramgate were all that my friend John had promised and more, and the four of us had a great time. I spent about fifty pounds on 'new' clothes, including a superb black and white hound's-tooth check sports jacket from Oxfam, a fiver, which complemented perfectly the pair of charcoal grey Daks slacks I acquired from SCOPE - Atkins said I would look like a bookie but I think he was a bit jealous because I'd spotted the jacket before he had - and the others spent about the same.

Despite my telling him that John was probably joking when he'd mentioned that a good way of dealing with students was to poke them with an umbrella Atkins, lacking an umbrella, had brought along a cricket stump. Happily we experienced no problems with students so he had no need to poke them with it; much to his disappointment, I might add, as he said he quite liked the idea of poking a student as it was a student who had recently poked his granddaughter and put her in the family way before going up to Cambridge and leaving her in the lurch.

Ironically the only problem we had in this regard was when Atkins and Harrison both went for the same pair of trousers. Harrison claimed he had laid hands on them first, a claim hotly disputed by Atkins. The matter was resolved only when Atkins pointed out that not only was he the driver of the car that had conveyed all of us to York, but would not necessarily be conveying all of us back, but he also had a cricket stump that he was itching to try out, whereupon Harrison reluctantly let go his grip on the trousers and Atkins bought them for £3.50, a bargain.

After we had gorged ourselves on all that the charity shops had to offer and had stowed our purchases in the boot of Atkins's car, Atkins and I made our way to the Jorvik Viking Centre, as planned. Harrison and Hargreaves had chosen not join us, claiming they'd already seen the Viking Centre a couple of years ago and apart from that they'd had more than their fill of Scandinavians what with ABBA. Atkins, perhaps getting the wrong end of the stick, asked them if they played ABBA records at the Viking Centre as he wasn't all that keen on them either and might forego the experience of seeing a long boat if it meant he had to put up with hearing 'Waterloo' and 'Dancing Queen' again, but Hargreaves assured him they didn't. So we agreed to meet back at the car later and went our separate ways.

At least one of the separate ways that Harrison and Hargreaves went led to a pub, because when we met up with them some two hours later they were both the worse for drink. Another of the separate ways they went was to the banks of the River Ouse where, no doubt due to his inebriated condition, Harrison had tripped and staggered into the river almost up to his waist.

If he had fallen into the river headfirst and wet his top half it would have been fine, for Harrison's purchases from the charity shops had included a variety of shirts, sweaters, waistcoats, jumpers and jackets. However he had not bought any trousers, the only pair he fancied having been bought by Atkins, as explained earlier. Atkins, who can be quite uncompromising if you get on the wrong side of him, was all for making Harrison travel all the way home in wet trousers until I pointed out that if he were to do this he would leave the back seat of the car wet-through and smelling of the River Ouse for weeks, something which Mrs Atkins might have a thing or two to say about. Atkins, Harrison and I had all purchased charity trousers so clearly a loan of a pair of them to Harrison was the solution.

Hargreaves is a much smaller man than Harrison so any trousers he had purchased would clearly be unsuitable, and both Atkins and I, whose trousers would be approximately the right size, were reluctant to loan them to Harrison. In the end we tossed-up for it, and Atkins lost. Atkins, true to form, demanded the best out of three, which I acceded to, and won again, but when he then demanded the best out of five I demurred. Harrison went into a gents' toilet to change into the trousers. When he emerged I remarked how smart he looked in them and what a perfect fit they were. Atkins gave me a dirty look and warned Harrison to look after them and treat them with respect. Some hopes.

All went smoothly on the return journey until we had been travelling for about an hour, Atkins and I chatting about this and that and listening to the radio whilst Hargreaves and Harrison slept off their booze in the back seat. Then suddenly, about a couple of miles after passing through Penistone and entering the bleak moorland of that area, Harrison awoke, farted loudly and shat himself. "Bloody hell I've filled my trousers!" he announced, totally unnecessarily, for the smell was both immediate and appalling.

Atkins stopped the car and turned to Harrison. "You dirty, smelly-arsed twat," he said. I couldn't have put it better myself, although I might have added a few more expletives.

"Sorry," bleated Harrison. "I'll pay you for the trousers of course."

"Too bloody right you will," said Atkins. "Now get out of the car and take them off, I'm not putting up with that stink for another twenty odd miles."

"I can't sit here without trousers," protested Harrison, rather primly, considering what he'd just done.

"Nobody's asking you to sit there without trousers," said Atkins. "So shut up and do exactly as I say. Get out of the car. Take off the trousers you have shit in. Go to the wall at the side of the road and throw them in the field. Try not to hit a sheep. Then go to the boot of the car, which I will open for you, take out another pair of my charity trousers, put them on, and get back in the car."

Harrison got out of the car and did exactly as Atkins had instructed him until he got as far as going to the boot of the car, whereupon Atkins, instead of opening it for him, set the car in motion in a fair imitation of the driver of a getaway car in a bank robbery, leaving Harrison stranded and trouser-less in the middle of the road.

"That'll teach the bastard to shit in my trousers," said Atkins.

Hargreaves, who by now had also woken up and taken an interest in the proceedings, protested. "You can't just leave him in the middle of the moors!"

But Atkins could. And did. Like I said, Atkins can be quite uncompromising if you get the wrong side of him and shitting in his trousers is definitely not the way to get the right side of him.

Apparently, according to Hargreaves, who I rang later for possible news of his friend, Harrison had eventually been given a lift back by the driver of a passing car, but only after about fifty cars had refused to stop for him, presumably because he was wearing a sweater, socks and shoes but no trousers, a bizarre outfit even for Yorkshire. Even then he had only managed to obtain a lift after assuring the driver of the car that he wasn't a sheep-shagger, and after offering him twenty pounds for his trouble. Serve him right too.

****

June 1 2006. *COUNTDOWN.*

That toe rag Ron Atkinson was in Dictionary Corner on Countdown this week. I didn't watch it, but I hope it went like this....

THE COUNTDOWN STUDIO. THE URBANE <u>DES LYNAM</u> ACCOMPANIED BY THE UBIQUITOUS <u>CAROL VORDERMAN</u> ARE IN THEIR USUAL PLACES, ALONG WITH <u>RON ATKINSON.</u>

DES: And now for a little light diversion from the normal Countdown fare; a special game for our special guest for the week. Consonant please, Carol.
CAROL: N.
DES: Consonant.
CAROL: G.
DES: Another consonant.
CAROL: R.

DES: Vowel.

CAROL: I.

DES: I'll try another vowel please.

CAROL: And that one is E.

DES: And a final consonant.

CAROL: And we complete the word with another G. So that's N..G..R..I..E..G.

RON: That's only seven letters.

DES: Six actually, Ron. Now all you have to do is arrange them into a well-known word. At least a word well-known to you, that is. And here's a clue - it isn't 'Ginger'. And your time starts....now!

RON: Er....Greign?

DES: No.

RON: Ignerg?

DES: No. I'll give you a clue, Ron. It starts with an N.

RON: Nergig? Is Nergig a word?

DES: No. It starts N I G.

RON: Ngireg? I'm sure Ngireg is a word.

DES: No.

RON: Sorry then, no idea. So it looks like its early doors for me then.

CAROL: Oh I'm sure you can get it if you try, Ron.

DES: It starts N I G G E. You've only got one letter to put in.

RON: Sorry. No idea.

DES: Say the word, Ron.

RON: No.

CAROL: Say it Ron.

RON: Look you guys I've only just managed to worm my way back onto mainstream television, give me a fucking....give me a flipping break will you.

DES: Say the word Ron.

RON: No.

CAROL: Say it - and I'll promise not to appear on any other television programmes apart from Countdown ever again.

RON: Not even for that.

DES: Say it Ron, or we won't ever invite you back.

RON: Er….er….Ashley Cole.

DES: What?

RON: Well he's a nigger, isn't he….shit!

****

June 14 2006. *A BUDDING ENTREPRENEUR.*

Having not visited Yorkshire for ages I went again a few weeks after our York trip, this time to Sheffield to pick up a water pump for the garden pond. I chose to wear the sports jacket I'd bought in York, the one Atkins said made me look like a bookie. I asked The Trouble how I looked in it. She said, "You look like a bookie." I wasn't surprised; she shares the same star sign as Atkins, Capricorn the Idiot. Besides, there are worse people to look like than a bookie; in my experience bookies always look as prosperous as they actually are, which is very prosperous.

I managed to buy the water pump without anyone coming up to me and saying 'I want a fiver on Lucky Charm in the 3.30 at Redcar' and nothing else of interest happened worthy of comment until I stopped on the way back.

My trip took a little longer than expected and I'd started to feel a bit peckish as it was well past my lunchtime. The countryside route, partly through my home county of Derbyshire, was not short of hostelries offering pub grub - a Chef & Brewer, a Beefeater and a Happy Eater amongst them - but these places invariably promise more than they deliver, as I've found to my cost. Apart from that it always seems to take forever for your food to arrive and I wanted a quick fix. A tip - avoid like the plague any pub that advertises 'fare' spelt 'f..a..y..r..e'. If they can't spell the word 'fare' there's a very good chance they can't cook either.

Ahead of me I spotted a mobile snack bar parked up at a lay-by, the sort of thing at which lorries pull in, although there were none there at the moment. A sign said 'Hot Food, Cold Food'. Just the ticket, I thought, and drew in. The proprietor was at the hatch. He was wearing a relatively clean white overall and not scratching his belly or picking his nose or anything, always a good sign. There was no menu advertised so I asked him what he had to offer.

"Bacon barmcake, egg barmcake, sausage barmcake, bacon, egg and sausage barmcake," he rattled off.

"I was looking for something cold?"

"Sorry mate, haven't got anything cold."

"Your sign says 'Hot Food, Cold Food'," I pointed out.

"Yeh, ham barmcake, cheese barmcake, cheese and ham barmcake. But I've run out. Hot day, had a run on cold stuff," he said, then added, doing his best to make it sound tempting. "The bacon, egg and sausage barmcake is very nice."

"I don't doubt it for one moment," I said, "But it isn't cold, is it."

He thought about it for a short moment then said: "You could wait for it to go cold."

What enterprise! What ingenuity! I certainly wouldn't have got such a response if a branch of Chef & Brewer had run out of cold food, neither from the Chef nor the Brewer.

"Sorry sir, there's nothing I can do about it," said apologetically, rather than matter-of-fact, if I were lucky, but more probably I'd have got a silent and disinterested shrug of the shoulders. Not from this man though. His entrepreneurial skills had kicked in immediately the problem had presented itself, and he had overcome it with ease. Britain could do with more men of his ilk; they are to be encouraged.

I encouraged him. "A bacon, egg and sausage barmcake, please."

Not a second over two minutes later this Alan Sugar of the highways slid an orange-yolked fried egg onto the crispy bacon and plump pork sausage he had already placed on the bottom half of the barmcake, then joined the two halves together. Two minutes, mind. It would have taken at least half-an-hour at a Happy Eater and even then there'd have been something wrong with the egg, apart from its yolk being a sickly pale yellow.

"Don't blow on it," I admonished him.

"I was helping it to go cold," he explained, a little hurt.

Helping it to go cold! Alan Sugar? Here was another Richard Branson in the making! "That's all right, I'll have it hot," I said.

It was quite delicious too.

****

August 14 2006. *TEENAGE AFFAIRS.*

'Burton's old flame tells of affair at 14', screamed the headline in the Sunday Times.

It struck an immediate chord with me and I read on with great interest. The article told the story of author Rosemary

Kingsland, now 'an attractive woman in her early sixties', and of her clandestine affair with actor Richard Burton when she was only fourteen. Apparently nobody else knew about the romance at the time and she has told nobody since, but now she 'wants the truth to be known'.

In the absence of any corroborative proof of their liaison some people might consider Mrs Kingsland's revelations to be a bit iffy to say the least, especially as being a writer she could easily have made up such a story; however I am not one of them, not least because a similar thing happened to me in 1956 when I too was a fourteen-year-old.

At the time I had gone to stay with my Aunt Polly and Uncle John in Los Angeles for a while. Like most boys of my age at that time I was madly in love with Marilyn Monroe, so imagine my great joy when one day I happened to spot her in a Hollywood diner having a coffee. Shyly I approached her and asked her for her autograph. She was even lovelier in real life than she was on the silver screen. She was very friendly and unaffected and after we'd chatted for what seemed ages she asked me if I'd like to go back to her place for a coffee. I said that she'd only just had a coffee but she told me not to be silly. Ten minutes later we were making love on her big pink bed. Over the course of the next week we made love a further fifteen times. She told me that I was a very good lover, not quite as good as President Kennedy but better than Bobby, which I thought wasn't bad for a fourteen-year-old whose only previous sexual experience had been with his soapy hand whilst sat on the lavatory.

Our affair might have gone on for longer but one day when I had gone down to the drugstore to get a soda for Marilyn I happened to bump into Natalie Wood. I mean literally bump into her. As we picked ourselves up our eyes met and we were immediately attracted to each other and when my hand accidentally touched one of her breasts as we dusted ourselves off it was all that was needed to bring us together. Our affair started just five minutes later. Our intention had been to go to Malibu where Natalie had a beach property but we were so attracted to each other we couldn't wait and ended up on the back seat of her open top white-wall- tyre pink Cadillac at the side of the freeway, screened from prying eyes by a roadside billboard advertising Pepsi-Cola.

We eventually did make it to her beachside property where we spent the next four days making love and relaxing in the Californian sunshine. Four days might have become four weeks but on the fifth day, whilst I was taking an early morning stroll along the beach, guess who I should meet? Greta bloody Garbo. That's right, the same Greta Garbo who once ensnared Peter Cook. All thoughts of a life with Natalie were put on hold when Greta told me she wanted to be alone with me, and of course the moment she was alone with me we made love. We spent a blissful, passionate, six days together but then sadly it was time for me to return to England as I had exams coming up.

As is the case with Rosemary Kingsland and Richard Burton I have never told a soul about my affairs with three leading Hollywood film stars until now. Again as with Mrs Kingsland I was never seen with my lovers and nobody knew or found out about us. A final coincidence is that my lovers too are now dead and unable to either confirm or deny any affairs we may have had in the past. But Rosemary and I know the truth.

November 3 2006. *BEST BEFORE.*

There can't be many people who can boast that they have their own beefsteak maturers, but happily I am one of them. Actually everyone in the country has their own beefsteak maturers but very few of them are aware of it. Let me explain.

In my home town, as is the case in many other towns up and down the country, we have a Co-op Late Shop. Why it is called a Late Shop is a moot point. The majority of people, but by no means an overwhelming majority, maintain it's called a Late Shop because it stays open later than most retail outlets, in fact until 10 p.m. each day. Others however, Atkins and myself amongst them, hold that it's because the check-out queues move so slowly that whenever you shop there it makes you late for whatever you intend to do next. Atkins further maintains that the 'Late' part of the name is probably a synonym for dead, as the checkout queues are so long and inert that one could die whilst waiting in them. On one occasion when I was in a Late Shop queue I thought this had actually happened when the woman in front of me collapsed to the ground in convulsions, but it turned out she was a diabetic who had been in the queue for so long she'd missed her insulin injection.

However the Co-op Late Shops, for all their faults, and death by check-out queue is but one of them, have the saving grace of being superbly efficient steak maturers. They are not aware of this of course, otherwise they would immediately put a stop to it and make themselves inefficient in this regard too, so as to bring it in line with everything else they do. In the meantime though, for the reader who wishes to avail him or herself of their unbeatable steak maturation service, here's how you go about it: -

Never buy any of their cuts of steak at the full price. Wait until they reach their 'Best before' or 'Sell-by date' and have a 'Reduced to clear' sticker attached to them. By this time the steak will have lost the bright red colour it had when first put on the shelves about ten days previously and will now be a very dark red, almost black colour, fully matured and ready to eat. These steaks are not only very easy to come by but have the added advantage of having been approximately halved in price - typically a steak that started life at £3.99 will now be priced at £1.99.

One might be tempted to think that given the choice of un-matured bright red steak and matured dark red steak at half the price that people would jump at the mature steak. The truth is that the majority of people wouldn't buy the dark red mature steak at any price, as they equate its colour with the steak having gone off. In fact the reverse is the case as the dark red colour of the steak is the signal that it is now ready to eat.

Indeed the 'Best before' date is a misnomer and should if anything read 'Worst before'. This is not my opinion but a fact. Many years ago I asked the owner of an excellent restaurant how it was that his sirloin steaks were always so tender whereas the steaks at many other restaurants, and the steaks I cooked at home for that matter, were nowhere near as succulent. I suspected he had access to some secret outlet of superior steak but this turned out not to be the case, the steak he bought being of good quality but no better than could readily be obtained by anyone. He took me into his kitchen and through to a cool, dark pantry. Hanging on hooks from the ceiling were thirty or so full sirloins and other cuts of steak. They ranged in colour from bright red to almost black. "These are fresh in," he said, pointing to the

sirloins. Then he indicated the ones that were
⸱k. "In about two weeks they'll be that colour.
they get to that colour, and not a moment before,
they'll be fit for the table."

I've never forgotten that lesson and over the years it must
have saved me hundreds of pounds. Not only that, it has
meant that the steak we have at home is always wonderfully
tender and juicy. So the next time you pass through the
butchery department of a supermarket and see steaks with a
'Reduced to clear' sticker on them don't turn your nose up at
them, snap them up. *Bon Appetite*.

****

November 17 2007. *AN EVENING WITH JOAN COLLINS*

In the Sunday Times Culture section yesterday I spotted an
advert in the forthcoming concerts pages - 'An Evening with
Joan Collins. UK Tour 2006. With special guests 4 Poofs
and a Piano'. Below the heading was a list of venues where
Miss Collins and the 4 Poofs, along with their piano, would
be appearing. I wondered briefly how the 4 Poofs have been
able to resist a slight change of musical instrument in order
that they might call themselves '4 Poofs and an Organ'.

Miss Collins's nearest port of call to me is Manchester
Bridgewater Hall on 10th May. I shan't be bothering. I've
already spent an evening with Joan Collins, or part of one.
Furthermore it wasn't as a member of the audience but
seated right next to her.

The occasion was when we were both guests, along with
others, on the radio programme 'Saturday Night at
Quaglino's', a live chat show that was broadcast in the early
eighties from Quaglino's night club in London's West End,

and hosted by Ned Sherrin. Whether Quaglino's, or indeed Ned Sherrin, is still around, I've no idea, but probably not.

I was on the show because at the time I was a scriptwriter on the News Huddlines and we'd recently published a book of scripts from the show. Along with another Huddlines writer Laurie Rowley I was there to plug it, which we did unmercifully and at every opportunity.

I'm not sure why Joan Collins was there, but the late Leonard Rossiter was a guest also (before he was late of course), so it might have been something to do with the Cinzano television commercials. I forget.

I was seated next to Joan, along with the other guests, at a large round table, set more-or- less in the middle of the night club where all the night clubbers could get a view of us. It crossed my mind that here might be an opportunity to progress from being a humble scriptwriter to a film star if I could impress Miss Collins in some way.

This was around the time of Joan's soft-porn movie 'The Stud', and it crossed my mind that if I were to perhaps unzip my fly and get my dick out under cover of the tablecloth and draw her attention to it she might consider me for a part in 'Stud 2'. Then I realised that if I were to do this it would be more likely to land me a role in a remake of 'The Smallest Show on Earth' so common sense prevailed and my trousers remained zipped.

This was over twenty years ago but I swear that Joan looked exactly the same as she does today. Dog rough. No, that's unfair, because I couldn't really say what she looked like due to the entire year's production of a small cosmetics factory having been trowelled on her face. She was white. Not just white, but white 'white'. A charitable person might say her faced looked like it had been fashioned out of

37

porcelain, an uncharitable one from Polyfilla. However she must have been over fifty at the time so I suppose she felt nature needed a helping hand even then.

As a person though she was charm itself, no edge with her at all, and I won't have a word said against her. Even though I never got to be in 'Stud 2'.

****

November 22 2006. *FORGETFUL.*

I am a few months shy of my sixty-sixth birthday and today is the first time I've ever been upstairs and forgotten what I'd gone up for. I've done surprisingly well by some accounts; it started happening to The Trouble before she was sixty and I know several people younger than me who it happens to on a regular basis.

"What are you stood there like that for?" said The Trouble, coming out of the bathroom.

"Like what?"

"Just stood there staring at the walls."

That was all I needed; she'd given me something I could build on. I built. "I was just thinking it was about time they were decorated," I said. Well I wasn't going to admit I'd forgotten what I'd gone upstairs for. It's the one thing I have over The Trouble in the 'things that happen to you when you're older' category. She's still got twenty/twenty vision, I have to wear glasses to read; she's still got all her teeth, I've got hardly any of mine; she's still got all her hair, ditto any of mine.

Of course my pride or vanity or whatever you want to call it is going to cost me whatever Hughes & Son, the painters and decorators we use, charge me for decorating the landing, because The Trouble instantly agreed with me and said she'd get them on the job right away. But then everything has a price, or, in the case of Hughes & Son, a fancy price.

When The Trouble went down the stairs I gave it a minute to remember what I'd gone up them for. I didn't remember it. I gave it another minute. I still didn't remember it. I did remember someone saying, Atkins I think it was, because it happens to him, that immediately you go downstairs again you remember what you went up for, so I went downstairs. Atkins doesn't know what he's talking about, as per usual, because I still didn't remember. The Trouble came out of the living room on her way to the kitchen. I went back upstairs again before she could ask me what I was doing stood at the bottom of the stairs and I managed to lie my way into having to have the hallway re-decorated along with the landing by the mercenary Hughes and his mercenary offspring.

I gave it a minute at the top of the stairs, in case the trip back up had jogged my memory and I remembered what I'd gone up for in the first place, but no such luck. I was determined it wasn't going to beat me. I knew if I gave in that it would just be the start of my going upstairs and forgetting what I'd gone up for - at my age I recognise a slippery slope when I come across one, alcohol, cigarettes, other women, so I was determined to beat it. I thought of all the possible things it could be that I'd gone up the stairs for. To change my shoes? For some money? For a book? I thought of about fifty things. None of which I'd gone up for. The Trouble came upstairs again. "I can't make up my mind between off white and avocado," I said, giving the walls a good coat of looking at prior to the exorbitantly-priced coats of paint Hughes & Son would soon be applying to them. "We're having it peach," she said.

I had to go back down again as I'd no excuse to be standing there now she'd sorted out the colour scheme but when she came down again I went back up again. An hour later, an hour's racking my brains, and I still didn't know what I'd gone up for.

The Trouble came back upstairs. I was just about to tell her I was having trouble with peach and would she compromise with primrose when she suddenly stopped and stood there, looking thoughtful. "Now what did I come up here for?" she said.

"You must be getting old," I said, and went back downstairs.

****

December 14 2006. *BLIND MEN.*

There aren't too many advantages in being old, and many disadvantages, but one of the few benefits that we coffin-dodgers have over younger people is that we can get away with things a lot easier as allowances are made for our advanced years. "Oh take no notice of him, it's his age," they say, in that condescending way, never for a moment suspecting that the artful pensioner might sometimes be using the cover of his age in order to get away with something that he otherwise might not have. Such as Atkins and I do when we play one of our daft games; because I'm quite sure we wouldn't be tolerated or excused as easily if, say, we were in our thirties. Take the game of 'Blind Men' we often play, and which we have never yet failed to walk away from without insult or assault being visited upon us,

40

where similar antics from younger people would probably bring down the wrath of the public on them. In fact I remember playing a version of Blind Men as a child and often receiving a slap round the ear-hole for my pains. However the adult version of the game is a bit more refined, as indeed are Atkins and I.

We usually travel to Stockport or Buxton, and Manchester on one occasion, to play it, as we're too well known in our own little town and probably wouldn't get away with it so easily.

It all went off as usual. Armed with white sticks we stood at opposite sides of a busy street, facing inwards, as though waiting for someone to help us across the road. And as usual someone soon did. Quite often a helpful man or woman will stop to help me before one stops to help Atkins, or vice versa, and when this happens, and for our game to work properly, we have to take delaying action by engaging our knight in shining armour in conversation, such as "You're quite sure there's nothing coming are you, because I wouldn't like to be knocked over at my age?" or "Can you hold on a minute I'm going to sneeze, now where did I put my hankie?" That sort of thing.

However today we were fortunate enough to get a willing helper at the same time. Holding onto our guides by the arm we each set off on our journey across the road, tapping our white sticks on the road the while, then, when we met in the centre of the road we suddenly shrugged off our helpers, brandished our white sticks high in the air as though they were swords, and took up fencing stances.

"On guard, you French scum," I demanded of Atkins.

"Hah! You weel soon feel the cold steel of my sword you Eenglish peegdog!" retorted Atkins.

Then we started fencing with our white sticks. It stopped the traffic of course, as usual, and a sizeable crowd soon gathered.

Actually we're getting quite good at it now; not to the standards of Douglas Fairbanks Junior and Errol Flynn maybe but certainly as good as Kevin Costner when he was Robin Hood, so we put on quite a decent show. After a couple of minutes or so of cut and thrust we simply packed it in and just walked away together chatting amiably, lest we got into trouble with Plod.

Atkins once suggested that after a minute or so of fencing we should go round with the hat but I managed to talk him out of it; I'm not hard up enough yet to resort to begging, but perhaps it's one for the future. Another suggestion from a friend at our local was that it might be an idea to take it to the Edinburgh Festival as apparently street entertainment such as our 'Blind Men' is a popular feature there. Atkins was very keen on the idea and said that if we do go we should definitely go round with the hat, if only to cover our expenses. However I remain unconvinced, either of taking it to Edinburgh or going round with the hat. But if anyone reading this, especially students, would like to perform 'Blind Men' at Edinburgh, please feel free. Anything to keep you out of the charity shops.

****

January 10 2007. *EXCESS WEIGHT.*

Like most of us The Trouble tends to put on a few pounds over Christmas and the New Year and also like most of us she has ambitions to get rid of the surplus poundage as soon as possible. She happened to mention to me that this year she would have to do without the benefit of a set of scales in this annual quest to get back to her previous weight as unfortunately she had forgotten to weigh herself prior to the start of the festivities. No matter, she said, she would know when her weight was back to normal as the week before Christmas she had bought a new pair of trousers that fitted her perfectly. Her plan was to diet until the trousers fitted her as perfectly again. Foolproof. Not so. A sound method on the face of it, but open to abuse. I abused it.

I have a sister who, along with a sewing machine and the seamstress skills to go with it, shares my sense of humour. Just for a laugh I had her take in the waist of The Trouble's new trousers by a couple of inches. This morning The Trouble declared that she felt she had lost enough excess poundage to get into the trousers again and disappeared upstairs to our bedroom. I have never heard the howl of a banshee, but if it is half as terrifying as the noise that came out of our bedroom two minutes later then if banshees ever hit town I don't want to be around when it happens. I ran upstairs. The Trouble is not a fat woman, on the contrary she has a nice figure for her age, but even a nice figure cannot get away with an attempt to force it into a pair of trousers deficient in the waist measurement by two inches. Consequently the small amount of fat she normally carries round her waist had become a roll of fat spilling out of the top of the trousers, which, if not of lifebelt proportions, certainly looked like something which could be an aid to buoyancy had she been drowning.

Naturally I started to laugh. Not for very long though because she was clearly upset, which became clear to me when she threw a pot of Oil of Olay at me. I apologised, then in an effort to restore the good humour she had been in before she tried on the trousers I let her in on my little joke, adding as a bonus that she had probably reached her target weight after all. For some unknown reason she failed to see the funny side of it and she hasn't spoken to me since.

****

January 21 2007. *SHITHOUSE.*

A few days ago there was an item on the BBC one o'clock news about a road death. Distraught parents lamented the loss of their seventeen-year-old child, the victim of a hit and run. She was a lovely girl, bubbly, everybody liked her. Two days later, on the evening news, a man had spoken of his soldier son, killed in action. He had been a son to be proud of, brave, a lion, looked up to by his men, they would have followed him anywhere. And on yesterday's news a woman had told of her brother, shot dead when accidentally getting caught up in a drugs war. The victim had been really genuine, always had a smile on his face and a good word for everyone, would have given you his last penny, a veritable saint.

This morning I attended the funeral of The Trouble's cousin Norman. The service started with the congregation singing The Old Rugged Cross, Norman's favourite hymn according to the vicar, although how he knew I've no idea since the last time Norman entered a church prior to entering it feet first was when he got married. When someone got up to read the eulogy I thought we'd gone to the wrong funeral because the man of whom he spoke sounded like a cross between Francis of Assisi and Nelson Mandela with a bit of Little Lord Fauntleroy thrown in, and not at all like the

44

mean-spirited bigot I knew Norman to be. Indeed he was made out to be just as bubbly, genuine and saintly as had the people on the TV news who had died.

It struck me then that nobody who dies is a shithouse. Everyone is a smashing, wonderful person. No one dying is a swine, a coward, a tight-fisted vindictive twat who wouldn't give you the dirt from under their fingernails and who went around kicking cats for fun. I reflected that if a Martian had only television reports of the deaths of loved ones with which to form an opinion of Earthlings he could be forgiven for believing there wasn't a single arsehole in the whole world.

The conclusion to be drawn from this is that only the good die, shithouses never. So, in an effort to live as long as possible, I have decided to become a shithouse. Starting today. I informed The Trouble and Atkins of my intention, and the reason why. Atkins said it sounds like a good idea and that he may very well become a shithouse himself (I sometimes think he's well on the way). The Trouble said I should have no trouble whatsoever becoming a shithouse if my behaviour the other week is anything to go by. I assume she means the business with her trousers.

****

February 12 2007. *JUNK MAIL.*

I caught up with my junk mail return service today. I suppose I should know by now but it still never ceases to amaze me just how much of this unwanted garbage lands on my hall floor. It's only four weeks since I last dealt with it and there must be fifty letters at least. When you take that over a year, and add to it the supermarket flyers, carpet

45

cleaning offers, Wicks catalogues, freebie newspapers, election leaflets and sundry other bumf that infiltrates my letter box and pollutes my hallway it amounts to a lot of paper.

At first I used to content myself with merely dropping it in the waste bin. Later I took to opening it, discarding the contents, sealing up the pre-paid reply envelope found inside and posting it back to from whence it came. This of course meant that the companies who sent me the junk mail ended up paying the postage on the letter whilst have nothing to show for it, at the same causing the pendulum to swing my way a little.

Recently I refined the service and now the pendulum swings even farther in my direction. I now open two junk mail letters at a time, take out the contents, put the contents of letter 'A' into the pre-paid reply envelope from letter 'B', and vice versa, then send them back. I've no idea as to the reaction of the person at the other end who opens them. Probably apathy. But then *I* don't care, either.

A refinement of the above idea, which I have amused myself with quite a few times, is to actually fill in the order forms of offers and return them in the wrong envelopes. Except for my credit card details, which I falsify just in case, I fill them in absolutely correctly, age, address, where to leave the parcel if I am out, etc. For example the other week I received in the same post a plant catalogue and the offer of the latest in deaf aids. I ordered four dozen daffodil bulbs from the deaf aid people and two deaf aids from the plant catalogue people. I have yet to receive a reply from either. You might think that the plant catalogue firm, having received an order for two deaf aids, would pass the letter on to the deaf aid people, but no, apparently plant catalogue

46

companies are only interested in selling plants; you could be as deaf as a post for all they care so long as you buy a hundred onion sets or a bag of early cropping seed potatoes.

Similarly you might suppose that the deaf aid company, having wrongly received an order for four dozen daffodil bulbs, would see to it that the order reached its correct destination. After all there is a good chance that the man who sent the order is deaf, so you wouldn't expect them to knowingly withhold from him the joy of seeing his daffodils blossom come next spring even if he'll never have the pleasure of hearing them gently rustling in the breeze. But again, no.

It isn't just the plant catalogue and deaf aid companies that are so cold and uncaring; since I started doing it I must have sent at least a couple of dozen orders to the wrong address and I have yet to hear so much as a whisper from any of them. Seemingly there is zero liaison between companies, who are apparently only interested in selling their own goods. Well cut my legs off and call me Shorty!

I have yet to meet the person who likes receiving junk mail, so with this in mind here's a thought - why not take a leaf out of my book and do as I do? There's no need to go to the trouble of swapping over the contents of the envelopes - although it is very satisfying and can be highly recommended - just send the empty pre-paid envelope back. If everyone were to do this there would be no junk mail at all after about twelve months. Bliss.

****

February 14 2007. *MY FUNNY VALENTINE.*

Every time Valentine's Day comes around with it comes messages of undying love from couples so besotted with each other that they seemingly don't mind calling their partner, and being called by their partner, the most ludicrous names.

A brief look through the columns of just one of the three pages my newspaper devoted to these missives of love revealed all the usual suspects. Honeypots and Honeybuns abounded, as did Sweetpeas and Cheekychops. Gladiator, Spartacus and Hercules represented both the historical and film worlds. Popeye, Goofy and Cartman the world of cartoons. The Animal Kingdom fetched up with a Squirrel Nutkins, seven Tigers, two Piggywiggies, a Lion, a Wilderbeast (sic), a Slimy Slug (sick), a Dobbin, a Mr Toad, the twosome of Mr Leghorn & Broodyboos and an Eager Beaver (although as this was a woman it could of course have referred not to an animal but something else). We also had, unfathomably, a Mr Sock, and a Huggy Buggy, The Perminator (must be a hairdresser), a Tubbyblubbyhubby, and the inspired pairing of Janey Fatbum & Spanker, which sounds to me like a match made in heaven. I'll draw a veil over the homosexual fraternity, other than to say that they were well represented, and I thought that the partnership of Jimmy Tightbum and Dyna Rod to be almost as well-matched as that of Janey Fatbum and Spanker.

Why do people call each other such names? More to the point, *how* can they call each other names like this? And is it only in the privacy of their own love nests, or do they refer to each other in this manner when they're out, and in company? "So that's a pint of bitter for me, a gin and tonic for Squidgypots, a pint of lager for Toddy Tiddler, a bacardi

48

breezer for Minxy Moo, a scotch for Bunny Wunny Wabbit and a slimline tonic for Fatarse."

It all reminds me of a sketch I once wrote for my radio series Star Terk Two, in the eighties.

A NEWSAGENTS SHOP. DAVE WALKS UP TO THE COUNTER WHERE THE NEWSAGENT IS SERVING.

DAVE: Could I put a Valentine's Day message in next week's Advertiser, please?
NEWSAGENT: Of course. What would you like to say?
DAVE: 'To my darling Jenny, lots of love, Dave.
NEWSAGENT: (WRITES IT DOWN) 'To my darling Jennypoos, lots....'
DAVE: Jenny.
NEWSAGENT: What?
DAVE: Just 'Jenny'.
NEWSAGENT: No 'poos'?
DAVE: No.
NEWSAGENT: It isn't any extra.
DAVE: I don't want a 'poos', thank you.
NEWSAGENT: Suit yourself. (WRITES IT DOWN) 'To my darling Jenny, lots of love, Davey Wavey.
DAVE: Dave.
NEWSAGENT: Pardon?
DAVE: Just Dave. And another thing, you don't spell 'lots of love' like that.
NEWSAGENT: You do. (SPELLS IT OUT) L..O..T..Z..A..L..U..V. Lotzaluv.
DAVE: Yes well when I went to school it was three separate words, 'Lots', 'of' and 'love'. So I'd like it like that, please.

NEWSAGENT: Well you're the one who's paying I suppose. So that's 'To my darling Jenny....megasqidgeons of love, Dave'.

DAVE: 'Lots' of love.

NEWSAGENT: 'Megasquidgeons' is another way of saying 'lots'.

DAVE: Not on my Valentine's Day message it isn't.

NEWSAGENT: 'Oodles of squidgeons of love'?

DAVE: *'Lots'* of love.

NEWSAGENT: 'Lots of squidgeons of....?

DAVE: Just 'Lots of love'!

NEWSAGENT: Right. 'To my darling Jenny, lots of love, Dave....(UNDER HIS BREATH)...ey diddle dum doos.'

DAVE: What?

NEWSAGENT: Nothing.

DAVE: What's that you've written down?

NEWSAGENT: What you told me.

DAVE: Let me see. Move your hand....My name is not Davey diddle dum doos!

NEWSAGENT: Oh come on, this is a Valentine's Day message; people always use silly names for Valentine messages.

DAVE: Well I don't.

NEWSAGENT: Oh lighten up for God's sake, it's only a bit of fun.

DAVE: No it isn't, using silly names is stupid and childish. So I'll just thank you to put 'To my darling Jenny, lots of love, Dave'.

NEWSAGENT: Very well then, if you insist. (WRITES IT DOWN) 'To my darling Jenny, lots of love, Dave.

DAVE: Thank you.

NEWSAGENT: And your full name and address please?

DAVE: Mr Dave Droopydrawers, 22 Acacia Avenue....

****

March 14 2007. *TREE SURGEONS.*

It's spring again, the time of year when you get men in green boiler-suits knocking on your front door asking you if you want any of your trees topped, lopped, felled or otherwise assaulted. The tree-felling close season is over and they're raring to go with their screaming chainsaws at the drop of a tenner. "That one needs to come down. What, tree that size? It wouldn't surprise me if the roots aren't right under your conservatory already, leave it much longer and your floor will be like the deck of the Titanic at iceberg time, just you see if it won't."

Tree surgeons are only marginally easier to get rid of than Irishmen who have some tarmac left over from a job up the road and who for a mere couple of hundred pounds will re-tarmac your drive with it to the depth of the thickness of the walls of a condom.

A few years ago, tired of the annual intrusions of the tree-fellers, I devised a plan to rid myself of them with the minimum of fuss. I would simply tell them that my house was for sale, and I was therefore not about to spend any money on it as obviously this would only be to the benefit of the new owner. It had always worked like a charm. Until yesterday.

"Good morning sir, Ace Tree Surgeons," the ace tree surgeon on my doorstep announced. "Do you want any of your trees' branches pruned or trees felling?"

On his green boiler-suit, underneath the letters Ace Tree Surgeons, was a little motif of a tree surgeon at work on a

51

tree, should I think he was a man from Mars. As he went through his opening spiel the ace tree surgeon was expertly eyeing our small oak tree and no doubt the probable distance of its roots from our conservatory.

"Sorry, we're moving house," I said.

"Oh," he said, disappointed.

He almost went, but then turned and stood his ground, clearly not completely happy with my excuse. "Where's your sign?"

My reply was the old standby of a person found out in a lie. "What?"

He pointed across the road to the 'For Sale' notice planted on the Rigby's front lawn. "Your 'For Sale' sign? Where is it?"

My first thought was to tell him that a tree surgeon had cut it down yesterday in mistake for my oak tree whose roots were about to undermine the floor of the conservatory, but he was a big bloke and I wasn't at all sure he'd appreciate the wit of this cutting riposte. "Kids stole it," I said, "Little sods will pinch anything round here." and closed the door quickly before he offered to massacre them for me with his chainsaw, only a tenner.

****

April 3 2007. *PETER KAY.*

About a couple of months ago I wrote some comic material, some short routines, and sent them to Peter Kay via his agent. I hadn't done any scriptwriting for ages but I was inspired to after my daughter had loaned me some of Peter Kay's CDs, one of which was 'Live at Bolton Albert Hall', which I had enjoyed enormously. A funny man, Peter Kay.

Performing the sort of material I could write. I wrote. There follows an extract from one of the scripts I sent to him, selected not because it's the best one but because it's the one about being old.

.....I mean you can't set foot outside the house nowadays without bumping into about two dozen old people in a walking party. Why can't they stop in and sit in the corner smelling of mothballs and trumping like they used to? (PULLS A FACE, WAFTS AWAY A SMELL. CALLS) *'Get some more moth balls when you go out would you, Dorothy'. But no, they're all out there, in the gear - bob hat, waxed jacket, corduroy trousers, waterproof leg bindings, map, compass, binoculars, haversack, one of them special walker's sticks with a spike in the end and enough equipment for an assault on Everest - and they're only going for a half-mile walk along the canal. They used to call it rambling. They should still call it that because they all ramble.... 'Nice here isn't it'.... 'Lovely. Not as nice as Turkey though'.... 'What?'..... 'Not as nice as Turkey'.... 'Right. Although given the choice I'd always have chicken .....'*

You can tell the leader because he's got a beard and more badges on his waxed jacket than the others. (WALKS SMARTLY ON SPOT, TURNS TO CALL BEHIND) *'Try to keep up will you.'*

'It's these new boots.'

'Did you treat them with dubbin like I told you?'

Hey, that brings back memories, dubbin. When I were a kid we used to have to rub it into our football boots - when football boots were football boots, not these carpet slippers they wear nowadays. 'And Giggs is running down the wing with the ball seemingly stuck to his feet.' If he'd rubbed about a pound of dubbin into each boot like we had to the ball it would be stuck to his feet. The problem wasn't getting the ball to stick to your feet it was trying to get it off once it had stuck there. There was no blasting it into the net from the edge of the penalty area in those days, if you wanted to score you had to run into the net. (HE RUNS PONDEROUSLY, DRAGGING ONE OF HIS LEGS, AND THROWS HIMSELF INTO AN IMAGINARY GOAL. THEN DETACHES AN IMAGINARY BALL FROM HIS FOOT AS THOUGH IT WERE AS HEAVY AS A CANNONBALL, TOSSES IT AWAY IN TRIUMPH BUT WITH A GOOD DEAL OF EFFORT) *Well footballs were heavy in those days. Bend it like Beckham? If he kicked one of the footballs I used to have to play with the only thing that would bend would be his foot.*

'Well, did you treat them with dubbin then, like I told you to?'

'They didn't know what dubbin were at Tesco's. She said try t' deli counter. They'd never heard of it either so I bought an onion bahji.'

'Did you think of trying a shoe shop?'

'They don't have loyalty cards at t'shoe shop.'

'I'm tired, can we stop for a rest?'

'We'll be late for our bar snack if we stop, it's booked for twelve and we're already an hour behind schedule.'

'I hope they know I can't eat chips with my stomach.'

'I want to go to the toilet.'

'Why didn't you go before we set off?'

'I didn't want to go then.'

'I went before we set off but I want to go again, it's me prostate.'

'Have you tried rubbing dubbin on it?'

And so it goes on. 'Try to keep up' 'Can we stop for a rest' 'I want to go to the toilet' I reckon that once people reach the age of forty they mentally start to go back in years instead of forward so by the time they're seventy they're ten again. If a man is aged seventy nine it's like he's one year old again - no teeth, no hair and no control over his bodily functions. And once they get into their seventies they start being childish again. Telling tales about each other, that sort of thing. 'Her next door is behind with the rent again. And Hitler was alive when she last paid her poll tax. I believe she's thick with the postman as well'. They say that in Bolton, 'thick with somebody' when they mean friendly with them. They don't say 'thin' with them if you're unfriendly with them though. They say you're being a twat with them....'

I never got a reply. So about a month later I sent the scripts again, in case they'd got lost in the post. Nothing. I could believe they'd got lost once but not twice. I was disappointed, because even if Peter Kay had thought the scripts weren't the sort of thing he was looking for he could at least have had the grace to reply. I remember many years ago sending some material to Jimmy Tarbuck when I was trying to get started as a scriptwriter. He wrote me a very nice note back, saying thanks very much for my interest but he already had a couple of scriptwriters he was happy with.

A week or two later I played another of the CDs my daughter had loaned me. This one was from his first television series, 'That Peter Kay Thing'. About halfway through, talking about his birth, Peter's character said, "My mother was a long time in labour with me because it was two days before the doctor realised she still had her tights on." A very funny line. In fact just as funny today as it was when I wrote it for Les Dawson as part of his opening monologue for an episode of 'The Dawson Watch' we did about the National Health Service in 1979.

So apparently although my material wasn't good enough to warrant a reply, much less good enough to buy, it was quite good enough to steal. I wrote again to Peter Kay, saying as much. And guess what? I didn't get an answer again. I will say no more. Except that I still think he is very funny. But not thin with me.

****

April 27 2007. *THE OLYMPIANS.*

I've always believed that walking is the finest exercise you can have apart from sex, and like sex it can be perfectly free - unless you start buying special clothes and equipment for it and call it hiking or golf - and at the age of sixty-six I still walk five miles every day just for the sheer pleasure of it.

It was while I was out walking and passing through the local park on the way to the canal for one of my regular trips along its towpath that I chanced upon an abandoned Zimmer Frame at the side of the path.

It immediately struck me what an unusual thing it was to abandon. I can understand people throwing away prams, their owners having no further use for them once their children have learned to walk, but I would have thought once you have found you need a Zimmer frame to help you get around you'd need one for life. It crossed my mind that maybe its former owner had been suddenly cured by a faith healer and having no further need of it had dramatically cast it away, a bit like the cripple who, on being cured by Jesus, had taken up his bed and walked. Or perhaps it had simply been thrown away by someone who had taken delivery of a new, lighter, faster, aluminium, tungsten-tipped , you-must-have-the-very-latest Zimmer Frame? I don't know. Anyway it was there in the park and I found it.

You have to take your opportunities for a bit of fun when and where you find them so when I noticed a man of about my age approaching I picked up the Zimmer Frame, twirled it round my head a couple of times, and heaved it into the distance. It had not long since been announced that Britain had been granted the 2012 Olympic Games, and with it the Paralympics, and it was probably this, and the thought I'd just had about cripples taking up their bed and walking, that put the idea into my head.

After I'd gone to recover the Zimmer and started to walk back the man had stopped to watch, and now looked on, puzzled. I turned to him and said, a little self-critically, "Not bad."

His face was a picture of inquisitiveness. "What are you doing?"

"Training for the Paralympics."

"Paralympics?"

"Throwing the Zimmer Frame," I explained. "Apparently the host country can pick an entirely new event and Britain has chosen 'Throwing the Zimmer Frame'. It just nudged out the 'Hop, Hop and Hop for the One-legged' I believe."

I returned with the Zimmer to the spot from which I'd thrown it. Two twirls round my head and I launched it again. This time it went about five yards farther.

"Better," the man observed, encouragingly.

"Yes, must be close to my PB that one," I said, sounding pleased with myself. "That's Personal Best," I explained.

"Yes I know, I'm a fan of athletics," he said. He thought about it for a moment. "Can anyone enter?"

I shrugged as though I didn't really know. "Well I suppose. You'll need a Zimmer Frame of course." I had a thought. "It's possible you could qualify for a grant - you might be able to get funding for one if you show you any promise, I'm sure I've heard of pole-vaulters getting grants for fibre glass poles."

I retrieved the Zimmer and made to throw it again.

"Can I have a go?"

I handed him the Zimmer. He drew his arm back and threw it as hard as he could. It landed a good ten yards farther than my last effort.

"You're a natural," I said.

"Wasn't bad was it," the man said, pleased with himself. "For a first stab at it."

First stab at it! I had him hooked. I commenced to reel him in. "I tell you what," I said. "Why don't you get a Zimmer Frame of your own and join me? Apparently there's going to be an individual competition and a Pairs, one of you throws the Zimmer and the other one throws it back, sort of piggy in the middle but without the piggy. Then there's a team event, the four man lob - I think that involves passing on the Zimmer to the next thrower like a baton, but we'd need another two for that. I train every morning at ten."

He said he'd be there the following day, prompt.

Atkins, never a man to turn down the chance of a bit of fun, joined me for my next Throwing the Zimmer Frame training session at ten the following morning.

Ever resourceful, Atkins already had his own Zimmer Frame, having picked it up at a charity shop some time ago in readiness for when the time comes when he'll need one, and employed in the meantime in his back garden as a support for his climbing strawberries.

We arrived at the park to find that the man whom I met yesterday, Mr Jefferson it transpired, was accompanied by two of his friends, who were also interested in training for the Throwing the Zimmer Frame 2012 Paralympics event. They looked to be aged about seventy. One was introduced as Mr Barnaby, the other, a Scot, was Mr Ross. It turned out that Atkins knew Mr Jefferson. He had been Atkins's milkman years ago before he ran off with a woman from across the road - Mr Jefferson that is, not Atkins - which had forced Atkins into making his milk arrangements with the Co-op. Atkins mentioned this to him, and that he had been left milk-less and strawberry yoghurt-less for a time, and Mr Jefferson apologised profusely. Atkins said there was no need to apologise, if he himself had been running off with the woman from across the road the last thing he would have had on his mind would have been someone's milk and strawberry yoghurt because she was a cracker. Mr Ross remarked what a small world it was, Mr Jefferson said it certainly wasn't big enough because the cracker's husband had found them and given him a right going over, and then we got down to some serious training.

Before we did this however Mr Barnaby felt constrained to point out that he didn't actually use a Zimmer Frame - the one he had brought along was his wife's - and enquired as to whether it was in the rules of the competition that a competitor had to be an actual Zimmer Frame-user, as if this was the case he didn't want to waste his time training up for the event only to be denied at the last moment. I confessed that I didn't know but asked him who was to prove otherwise? I also pointed out that the Paralympic Games were over five years away and by then he could quite possibly be genuinely in need of a Zimmer Frame, as indeed might the rest of us. This seemed to satisfy him.

Before we got down to some serious training I added a refinement in the shape of an 8 feet diameter circle, rather like the circle one sees in the sport of 'Throwing the Hammer', which I painted on the grass with some white emulsion left over from when we had our bedroom ceilings decorated.

The training went very well, the only problem being that Mr Ross, who is a genuine Zimmer Frame user, fell flat on his face every time he threw his Zimmer Frame. I assured him that this wouldn't lead to disqualification as the rules stated that provided the competitor didn't step out of, or in his case fall out of, the circle, it would be deemed to be a fair throw.

In fact it was Mr Ross who threw his Zimmer Frame the farthest. I wasn't surprised by this, because of his country of birth, the Scots traditionally being very big on throwing things, hammers, cabers, tantrums, uppercuts, sickies and so on. Mr Barnaby wasn't far behind and I thought it would be interesting to see which of them eventually turned out to be the best thrower. Atkins was hopeless, but this was probably because it took him all his time to keep his face straight, let alone throw his Zimmer Frame any distance.

We ended the session by having a chat about the way ahead and decided to put in for lottery funding, to be taken up by Mr Barnaby. On the way home Atkins and I decided there was no way we could continue without cracking up and decided not to go again, or if we did, to view the proceedings from the cover of the trees.

I had imagined that would have been the end of it but a couple of days later I was tidying up the back garden when the back door opened and The Trouble, wearing her 'And what have you been up to now?' expression, called to me. "There are three men with Zimmer Frames at the front door."

I tried to look unconcerned. "Oh yes?"

"Why?"

I spread my hands. "Search me. Perhaps they're collecting?"

"Well if they're collecting Zimmer Frames they've had a lot of success. Anyway they're asking for you."

I went to the front door. Abreast of each other were Mr Jefferson, Mr Barnaby and Mr Ross. Standing behind their Zimmer Frames they looked like a small football crowd. How had they known where I lived?

"Mr Atkins told us where you lived," said Mr Jefferson, answering my unspoken question as though on cue. I made a mental note to give Atkins a piece of my mind the next time we met; they'd obviously called on him, Jefferson knowing where Atkins lived by virtue of his once being his milkman before he ran off with the cracker, and were now intent on making me have some of the earache they'd no doubt given him.

"Why haven't you been turning up for training?" demanded Mr Ross.

"And I hope you've got a better reason than Mr Atkins," said Mr Barnaby.

"Why, what did he tell you?"

"That his wife said she isn't going without strawberries for five years just so he can go to London in 2012 to make a fool of himself," said Mr Jefferson. "So what's your excuse?"

"I've decided to switch my event," I said. They said nothing, just stood there looking at me, obviously expecting me to tell them which event I'd switched to. I thought quickly. I had to be careful; I didn't want to pick something they might want to change to because if I did that they'd probably rope me in to train with them. The Downhill Stairlift was the first paraplegic-sounding event that sprang to mind. Surely none of them would go to the expense of buying a stairlift? But hang on. Downhill Stairlift? Wouldn't that be a Winter Paralympics event? *Was* there such a thing as the Winter Paralympics? Skiing down the side of a mountain at a hundred miles-an-hour is difficult enough as it is without being hampered by having only one arm or one leg or partial sight, so probably not.

"So which event are you going in for then?" asked Mr Jefferson, breaking into my thoughts.

Fortunately inspiration came to my assistance. "Putting the Truss," I said. "In fact I'm just off to the hospital for a new one, nice seeing you all again," and with that I limped painfully down the drive and out of their lives forever. I hope.

****

June 10 2007. *FLATULENT CHAIR.*

There has been a lot in the newspapers recently about the teacher who sued her former school for £1 million in compensation after the school failed to replace her chair, which apparently made flatulent noises when she moved.

62

She was quoted as saying: "It was a regular joke that my chair made farting noises and I regularly have to apologise to pupils and parents that it isn't me, it's my chair." Many columnists, amongst them such luminaries as Richard Littlejohn and Keith Waterhouse, have put in their two pennyworth, but surprisingly for men of their eminence neither Littlejohn nor Waterhouse latched onto the most important feature of the case. Which is: is this woman stark-staring mad? Has she not considered the benefits of owning such a wonderful chair? For having established with her pupils and their parents that it is not she who is making the farting noises the woman can fart away to her heart's content, safe in the knowledge they'll think it's the chair. Just think of the fun she could have in class. She'd be able to pick out a particularly irksome pupil, let rip with a couple of ripe ones and say, "Who was that? Smells like one of yours, Jenkins. Write out 'I must not fart in class 1000 times and let me have it by morning at the latest'."

I don't know about demanding £1 million from the school, she should be paying them a £1 million for providing her with a chair like that.

****

June 14 2008. *THE REAL GREECE.*

Everyone, I'm sure, has seen the words many times in travel adverts or above articles by travel writers - 'Come to the real Spain' or 'Visit the real France' or 'Now enjoy the real Italy'. In today's Sunday Times travel supplement I saw another one, 'Visit the real Greece'. No thanks, I've tried it.

However I wouldn't mind visiting the unreal Greece, which would be a Greece where: -

The food served in the tavernas is hot, rather than something which has made its way from the kitchen to your table via the North Pole.

You can walk around town without your nose being assaulted by the stink of drains every few yards.

They don't have at least twenty different spellings of the word hamburger. Just three of many examples I've seen are humbleburger, harmburger and hambugger, which, although misspellings, were spot on as to the quality of the hamburgers in question.

Power cuts are the national sport.

You can walk past a restaurant without being accosted by a young Greek who is far better-looking than you and who implores you to step inside for 'many of our lovely foods' and won't take no for an answer.

You can dine outside without being up to the arse in stray cats.

You can put used toilet paper down the lavatory instead of having to put it in a bin overflowing with other used toilet paper.

There is a sporting chance of getting hot water in a reasonable quantity when you turn on the hot water tap.

They have plugs for the sinks so that you don't have to fashion one out of rolled up toilet paper which you then have to drop in a bin of used toilet paper because you can't flush it down the toilet when you've finished with it.

You can't hear exactly the same bouzouki music playing everywhere you go.

Cockroaches are looked upon as pets.

I'm sure there are many more examples of the real Greece but I have to stop now to cook a moussaka for dinner. Take a gallon of olive oil....

****

June 18 2007. *MARBLES.*

I had the most wonderful news today! Along with my monthly credit card statement from Marbles came the offer of 'Two nights away with the one you love for only £99.' The offer consists of a two night stay in any Hilton Hotel in Great Britain and Ireland, the price to include bed, breakfast, dinner on the first night, plus a complimentary bottle of house wine 'when you whip out your Marbles card!'

Thankful that my Marbles card would be all I will be required to whip out in order to qualify for my complimentary bottle of wine I rang them immediately, quoting the booking reference number as requested. "I'd like to take you up on your most generous offer of two nights away with the one I love for £99," I said.

"Very good, sir," said the man from Marbles, all obsequiousness and efficiency.

"Will Miss Scott Thomas be there when I arrive?" I asked him.

"Pardon, sir?"

"Kristin Scott Thomas. She's the woman I love. I've loved her ever since I saw her naked in 'The English Patient', what a body, all that pubic hair, like a forest, well I'm Jungle Jim so just lead me to it." There was a long silence at the other end of the phone. I broke it. "Hello? Hello, are you still there?"

The obsequiousness remained but the efficiency had taken a holiday, possibly a two night stay with the one it loved. "There....er, appears that there's some sort of misunderstanding, sir."

"Misunderstanding? You *are* offering two nights in a Hilton Hotel away with the one I love for £99 are you not?"

"Er....yes. But we mean your wife."

"My wife?"

"Or girlfriend."

"Your leaflet didn't say my wife or my girlfriend, it said the one I love," I pointed out to him.

"Yes....well....we assumed that a man's wife or girlfriend would be the one he loved," he bleated.

"That's a pretty all-encompassing assumption to make if you don't mind my saying so. Given all the divorces and extra-marital affairs and wife beatings one hears about nowadays."

He stuck to his guns. "Well that's what we meant, sir."

"Well then that is what you should have said. But you didn't. You said two nights with the one you love for £99. And if you don't see to it that I get two nights with the one I love, i.e. Miss Kristin Scott Thomas, she of the glorious beaver, for £99, I will sue Marbles for every penny it has got!" Then I put the phone down.

I don't love Kristin Scott Thomas of course, I love The Trouble'; although I quite fancy Kristin Scott Thomas and if anything should ever happen to The Trouble....

I suppose that will be the end of the matter. But it might not be. Even at this very moment the people at Marbles might be trying to contact Kristin Scott Thomas in an effort to help them to get out of the tricky situation they've landed themselves in with a dirty old man from the Peak District, just so the dirty old man won't sue them for every penny they make in exorbitant interest rates. Although probably not. But at least next time it might make them think before offering deals that they cannot possibly hope to fulfil.

****

July 24 2007. *THE BEST OF IT.*

I was feeling in a philosophical mood today and my philosophising led me to the conclusion, on comparing the world as it is today to how it was fifty sixty years ago, that I've had the best of it, that I was born into it at the perfect time, at a time when there were no such things as diversity and outreach officers, a time when a race card was a list of the runners and riders at Kempton Park and not something played by an ethnic minority to gain an unfair advantage, a time when people who ran banks were known as bankers not wankers.

I certainly wouldn't like to have been born now, despite all the advantages of inventions like television and computers and mobile phones, which weren't around when I popped out into the world, because along with all the televisions and computers came darker inventions like smart bombs and nuclear missiles and other abominations that can destroy the world in about five minutes flat, and probably will do before we're very much older.

And I wouldn't have liked to have been born very much earlier either, say a couple of centuries or so ago, because that would have landed me in an age when people got hung for stealing a loaf of bread, and if they managed to miss out on that probably died before they were thirty from the plague or rickets or scarlet fever or any of the countless other

67

diseases the medical profession had still failed to get to grips with. Amputation without an anaesthetic? Yes, I'll certainly take a pass on that.

Being born at the time I was my childhood was a joy, a magic time, an age when despite being born to mothers who drank and smoked like chimneys, in spite of the lack of childproof locks and childproof caps on bottles of pills and being allowed to play with lead toy soldiers painted with lead paint, regardless of the fact that we rode bikes without the need of more body armour than an American footballer and were allowed to eat white bread with butter on it and play conkers and climb trees which we fell out of from time to time because then there was no such thing as Health and Safety, and notwithstanding that we were allowed to stay out until dark without our mothers knowing where we were, we somehow all managed to survive intact.

And so we left school - but only after receiving quite a few hefty clouts round the head by the teachers, which didn't seem to have done us any harm and probably did us a lot of good - and then got a job, which I seem to remember was a much easier undertaking then, as nowadays you seem to require a university degree of not less than a 2.1 to even stand an outside chance of getting a job behind the counter at McDonalds.

Of course in those days you had to be clever to go to university, and if you happened to be one of the lucky ones you took a degree in Chemistry or Physics or English Language, unlike today where you don't have to be anything like so clever - you certainly don't have to be able to read and write any better than the average seven-year-old of my childhood - and along with subjects like Chemistry you can take a degree in Folk Music or Interior Decorating and quite possibly Advanced Train Spotting & Bungee Jumping. And it doesn't make a scrap of difference if something like Advanced Train Spotting & Bungee Jumping is the only degree you're capable of gaining you'll still probably end up at McDonalds dressed in a silly hat cooking French fries alongside the girl with a First in Economics.

And could I have chosen a better time to be a teenager? I don't think so. It was the era of the birth of rock and roll. We had Elvis and Little Richard, then a year or two later the Beatles and the Stones. What have the teenagers of today got? Rap. My parents used to complain that you couldn't tell what Mick Jagger was saying, nowadays not only can you not tell what they're saying you don't want to know what they're saying because it's usually all about stabbing each other, bro.

Even much later, when I was about fifty and this country had started to go pear-shaped, I could still pat a child affectionately on the head without the risk of being put on the sex-offenders register; if I caught a burglar breaking into my house, detained him by force and called the police it would be the burglar they locked up, not me; if I happened to take ill at weekend the doctor would come out and treat me, unlike today when I'm likely to be given the once-over by a moonlighting Albanian over for the weekend who can speak about as much English as our budgie; a time when the England cricket team still didn't win any more often than they do nowadays but at least more than half of them weren't born in South Africa; and when politicians, even in those days, were people you wouldn't trust as far as you could throw them, but were still a quantum leap better than the lying, thieving, self-serving excuses for human beings we

69

have representing our interests today. No, like I said, I've had the best of it.

Whew, glad I've got that off my chest. I might start to enjoy myself again now.

****

August 2 2007. *FENG SHUI.*

You would have thought that after seventeen years in our present home I would know the whereabouts of the bed, but no, for when I went to bed last night I walked straight into it. Naturally I hadn't switched on the bedroom light as I am under strict instructions from The Trouble not to do this whenever I turn in after her as it wakes her up and she can't get back to sleep, but that shouldn't have presented a problem as I've been finding my way to bed for some time now without the assistance of the North West Electricity Board or whatever fancy new meaningless name it calls itself nowadays.

Another factor which may have influenced matters was that I'd had one of my rare nights out at the pub with Atkins. At first it led me to believe I'd maybe had a little more to drink than was good for me, and that this was why I'd been unable to successfully navigate the two yards or so between the bedroom door and the bed. The truth is I did successfully it, or at least I would have done if the bed hadn't been rotated sixty degrees to the left.

"Feng Shui, and there's no need to swear," said The Trouble, after I'd picked myself up off the floor and asked her why the bloody hell the bed was where it was. "Having the bed facing east to west will ensure optimum happiness for the occupants," she blithely went on.

70

"Not if they can't find the way to it," I said, rubbing my shin where I had barked it on the bedpost.

"The trouble with you is that you won't make an effort to embrace other cultures," said The Trouble.

"Not other cultures that believe moving the bed will make a ha'porth of difference I won't."

I might have known of course. In the two days since The Trouble allowed herself to become influenced by the oriental claptrap that is Feng Shui she had already moved the three-piece-suite to a position from where it's impossible to see the television from my favourite chair without getting a rick in my neck and moved a standard lamp from a perfectly good position in the corner to a perfectly crap position just by the door where I keep walking into it every time I come in.

Normally The Trouble is one of the most level-headed and pragmatic of people who views the latest fads and fashions with a degree of scepticism, but a couple of years ago, shortly after she bought a wok, a Chinese acupuncturist cured her of a long-standing back problem. This, along with the fact that she claims to have felt a lot better since employing the wok to cook healthy stir-fry dishes, seemed to influence her judgement because from then on all Chinese beliefs, no matter how outlandish, were the bees knees, and soon the mysteries of Tai Chi and acupuncture and Yin and Yang had joined the mysteries of the local Chinese chip shop in our lives. I'm just glad that Mao Tse-Tung is no longer with us otherwise she might be quoting passages of his Little Red Book at me every five minutes.

"You'll soon get used to it," she said. "Think of the optimum happiness you'll soon be getting. Now turn off the light and get into bed and try not to snore too much."

71

I sighed and did as she bade me. She was right I suppose, I'd soon get used to the new position of the bed, but these things take time and I'd forgotten about it an hour later when I got up to go to the bathroom for my first pee of the night. Consequently, only half awake, I took the route to the bedroom door consistent with the bed's previous position. "Jesus Christ!" I screamed, as my big toe hit the dressing table. My scream would have awakened the dead, never mind a light sleeper like The Trouble, and she promptly woke up and switched on her bedside lamp. "Going to the bathroom," I explained. "Forgot our bedroom was a bloody assault course."

"You'll soon get used to it," she said for the second time that night, but now with a little less conviction. She was right though, because when I woke up about an hour later for my second pee of the night I clearly remembered there was a new route to the bedroom door. However by the time I'd had my pee, five minutes later, and made my way back to the bedroom I'd forgotten about it again. This time when I collided with the bed I didn't fall on the floor I fell on top of The Trouble, waking her up again of course. She snapped on the bedside lamp and looked up at me. I said the only thing it was possible to say in such a position: "Well since we find ourselves like this, how about making love?" And we did. And it ensured optimum happiness for me. But I don't think it had anything to do with the position of the bed.

****

72

August 10 2007. *DUCK.*

When I ordered duck I wasn't aware that Atkins couldn't abide other people eating it when he wasn't eating it himself. Not that it would have stopped me ordering it if I had known; far from it, I still haven't got him back for giving my address to the Zimmer Frame throwers.

There were eight of us at the meal to celebrate Ted Burrows' birthday; The Trouble and I, the aforementioned Atkins and his wife Meg, The Parsley-Hays, and Ted and his wife Caroline. The waiter had handed out menus and ten minutes later had asked each of us in turn what we would like. I was the last to be asked.

"Duck," I replied.

"Fuck!" said Atkins.

"*Sacre bleu*" said Caroline Burrows, who is learning French and tries it out at every opportunity.

"That means I'll have to have it now," Atkins complained.

"Have what?" said Ted Burrows, not having heard the foregoing exchange, being more interested in the wine list.

"Duck," said Atkins, his face like a wet week in Wigan. "I was going to have braised beef and savoury suet dumplings but now I'm going to have to have duck."

"He can't bear to see anyone eating duck when he's not having it," Meg Atkins explained to the rest of the party. "He can do *without* duck. He can cast duck completely from his mind. It could be as though there were no such creatures as ducks, as though ducks had never been on the face of the earth. But only if someone else isn't having duck."

73

"I was really looking forward to having braised beef and savoury suet dumplings as well," griped Atkins, giving me a dirty look.

The Trouble appealed to me. "Can't you have something else?"

"Well I could," I said, "but I'm in a duck mood."

"They have *bouef bourguignon*," coaxed The Trouble, "You like *bouef bourguignon*."

"No I'll stick to the duck if it's all the same to you."

"The guinea fowl in brandy and juniper berry sauce is excellent," cajoled Robert Parsley-Hay. "Jill and I had it the other week. It's very much like duck in fact."

"In that case I might as well have duck."

"It wasn't all that much like duck," said Jill Parsley-Hay, trying to retrieve the situation.

"No good for me then," I said, "I want something that definitely tastes of duck. Preferably duck."

"I thought you were supposed to be my friend!" accused Atkins. Atkins was once a member of the local amateur operatic society until they banned him and can get a bit melodramatic at times.

"Friend, not wet nurse," I said, sticking to my guns and my duck.

"I really had the taste for braised beef and savoury suet dumplings," moaned Atkins. "But now it's got to be duck."

"So why are you complaining then?" I said. "You like duck."

Atkins fumed. "I'm complaining because I fancied bloody braised beef and sodding savoury suet dumpling."

"*Calme toi, Monsieur Atkins, calme toi*," said Caroline, demonstrating her command of the French language, but not necessarily when to use it.

"Bollocks," said Atkins, demonstrating his command of the English language and exactly when to use it.

I decided to rack up a few brownie points to be cashed in at a later date. "Oh all right then. Anything for a quiet life. I'll have the *bouef bourguignon*."

Atkins was overjoyed. "Really?"

"I wouldn't have ordered duck in the first place if I'd known," I lied.

Meg Atkins was grateful. "Thanks, Terry."

Atkins added his gratitude.

The food arrived in due course. Atkins was the first to be served, with his braised beef and suet dumplings, and quite mouth-watering it looked too, in fact I wished I'd ordered it myself. The waiter served the rest of us. Last to be served was Ted Burrows. The waiter placed a plate before him. Sitting on it, invitingly, was half an extremely succulent-looking crispy-skinned duck smothered in a rich orange and whisky sauce.

"I ordered the pork medallions in cider," said Ted.

"Sorry, sir," said the waiter, making to remove the plate.

"No, it's all right," said Ted, "I quite fancy the duck now I've seen it, it looks quite mouth-watering."

"Fucking hell fire!" shouted Atkins, and without so much as another word got to his feet threw his knapkin onto the floor and stormed out.

We shared his braised beef and savoury suet dumpling between us. Well I had about half of it actually. It was as good as it looked.

****

August 17 2007. *BEARD*

This morning I happened to glance through the windows of the local gents' hairdressers. His price list caught my attention. It read as follows: -

MAN - £9.00
BOY TO 16 - £8.00
STUDENT - £8.50
OLD MAN 65-90 - £6.50
HEAD SHAVE 1,2,3,4 UP - £10.00
VERY OLD MAN 90 Plus - Negotiable
BEARD - £4.00
LONG BEARD - Negotiable
HAIR WASHED - £7.00
HIGHLIGHTS - From £15

I just had to go in. The shop was empty, except for the barber, who was reading the Sporting Chronicle whilst waiting for someone desirous of having a Head Shave 1,2,3,4 UP that would maybe supply the £10 for his £5 each way bet at Lingfield Park. On seeing me he immediately laid aside the Sporting Chron and sprang to his feet ready for action.

"Good morning. What will it be?"

"How long is a long beard?"

"A long beard?"

"Your notice says the price is negotiable. I'd like to negotiate ."

He looked at me closely with suspicious his eyes. "You haven't got a beard."

"I'm thinking of growing one. The thing is I'd quite like a long beard - a bit like one of the Gillette Brothers if you've

76

ever seen a photo of them, or maybe Karl Marx - but not if it's going to cost me substantially more than just a beard. I mean what's the cut-off price? If you'll pardon the expression. At what point does a Beard become a Long Beard?"

"Two inches is a Beard. After that it's a Long Beard."

"And how do you charge for a Long Beard?"

"Fifty pence an inch."

"So if I have a two foot beard it will cost me twelve pounds to have it trimmed."

"Right."

"What if I'm 90 Plus?"

"What?"

"Well if you're 90 Plus you get your hair cut more cheaply, I was wondering if that applies to Long Beards as well?"

"But you're not 90 Plus, are you."

"I will be by the time I've grown a two foot beard."

The barber looked at me even more suspiciously but after a moment said, "I'll knock you a couple of quid off."

"I'm a student too. Open University. Media Studies." I opened my wallet and flashed my bus pass. "My student's union card. A hair cut is cheaper for students; does that apply to beards too?....I can see from your face that it probably doesn't."

"Are you taking the piss, mate?"

"Not at all. So we'll leave it at that then shall we. Do I have to make an appointment? When I've grown my beard?"

"Fuck off."

"Right."

I fucked off. I wasn't about to argue the toss with a man who has access to a cut-throat razor.

August 24 2007. *SHIPMAN.*

A couple of years ago, whilst I was travelling by car to take part in a bowls match, one of my team mates pointed out a white painted stone cottage set a little back from the road. "See that house," he said. "That's where Shipman used to live." We were in the Gee Cross area of Hyde, Greater Manchester, and the Shipman in question was Dr Harold Shipman, the notorious mass-murderer who did for at least 218 and quite probably as many as 459 women between 1971 and 1998. I use the road fairly often and I've never been able to go past the house since without looking at it and I don't suppose I ever will, morbid curiosity getting the better of me as it does almost everyone.

Yesterday I returned to play bowls at the same venue, the Grapes Hotel. After I'd played my game I chatted for a while with my opponent, Ted Grundy, as we drank our pints of bitter. It turned out that Ted made his living as a house clearer. I asked him how was business? He said it was steady, and went on to tell me that, notwithstanding hypothermia in very cold winters, the house-clearing trade wasn't subject to great swings, there was always a steady flow of clients requiring houses to be cleared of furniture and effects. "Well usually," he added, with an odd smile.

I prompted him. "Usually?"

"Well in 1996 business suddenly started to go up. And stayed up. Not to a great extent, but enough to be noticeable. I didn't think too much about it at the time; I'd only been in the business a year or two and I thought maybe it was because I was doing a good job, that people I'd cleared houses for had recommended me to others. But it wasn't that, because a couple of years later it went back down again

78

as suddenly as it had gone up. And do you know why? I'll tell you. It was Shipman. It was at the height of his activity; he'd been murdering all these old women - and I'd been following him round a week or two later clearing the houses of those who had been living on their own! It was all down there in my records. The police file of the scenes of his crimes was my order book a month later."

It immediately dawned on me that if Ted had twigged on what was happening earlier he might have saved dozens of lives but I wasn't going to mention it, the poor bloke might not have been able to live with himself if he thought that. Eerily, as though he had read my thoughts, Ted said, "If I'd have twigged on earlier I might have saved dozens of lives

"Right," I said. Obviously he could live with this knowledge.

"Of course," he said, "whether I'd have told the police is another matter."

What did he mean, 'if I'd told the police'? Why would he not have told the police?

"I mean if the police had collared him earlier my business would have suffered," he explained.

And then he cracked a smile, informing me that he was only joking. At least I think he was only joking.

****

September 13 2007. *MR WOO*

Yesterday, six weeks to the day since our bed was given the Feng Shui treatment, the well-upholstered blonde who had talked The Trouble into going along with all this Feng Shui nonsense in the first place arrived at our house along with the Chinaman who had talked the well-upholstered blonde into going into it. The purpose of their visit was to check whether The Trouble had placed various items of our furniture in the most conducive positions according to the dictates of Feng Shui.

I wish The Trouble had warned me beforehand as it would have saved me the embarrassment of walking in on them in just my boxer shorts on my return to the bedroom after my morning shower.

"This is Mr Woo," said The Trouble, indicating the Chinaman, presumably in case I might be thinking the well-upholstered blonde was called Mr Woo.

"Shouldn't he be outside cleaning the windows?" I asked.

"Cleaning the windows?" said the well-upholstered blonde, officiously. "Why should Mr Woo be cleaning the windows?"

I gave her a quick burst of George Formby's Chinese Laundry Blues, accompanying myself on air banjo: "*Oh Mr Wu, what shall I do, I'm feeling kind of Limehouse Chinese Laundry Blues.*"

That was Mr Wu," said The Trouble, with a 'u'. "This Mr Woo spells his name W..O..O."

"Oh, Mr Wooooo," I said. "Like a puffer train."

"No, Woo," said the well-upholstered blonde.

"Take no notice of him," said The Trouble, then, to me: "Mr Woo is a Feng Shui expert."

Mr Woo smiled at me. "Nice underpants."

"You're not moving them," I said, my hands going involuntarily to the sides of my boxers.

"Mr Woo has come along to check if your bed is in the correct place," explained the well-upholstered blonde.

"I can save him the bother then," I said. "It is in the right place. In the bedroom. Where else would you put a bed, in the greenhouse?"

"You're embarrassing me," said The Trouble, giving me a look that would have frozen Birds Eye's annual production of peas.

"I'm embarrassing *you?"* I said. "I walk into our bedroom in just my boxers to find you and your barmpot of a mate and a Chinaman who looks suspiciously to me like the one who keeps the Chinese chippy on Market St and *I'm* embarrassing *you?"*

The well-upholstered blonde immediately leapt to the Chinaman's defence. "He doesn't look suspiciously like the one who keeps the Chinese chip shop," she glowered. "He is the one who keeps the Chinese chip shop. He is multi-talented."

"He is not," I said, "he can't cook chips for a start, he's fucking hopeless at it, they're always soggy."

I had overstepped the mark, of course. Although the F-word now seems to be more or less compulsory in conversation between the sexes when spoken by the young it is still taboo for people of my generation when in the company of women. (Except in London of course, or when you are in the company of just your wife and no other word will do.) My choice was simple. I could apologise or face the silent treatment for God knows how long. I apologised.

After much deliberation and tut-tutting Mr Woo moved the bed about two degrees to the north. Having spent a night in it I can't say I felt any happier in it. However The Trouble said she felt much happier in it and that the two degrees had made all the difference. I said that if the Three Degrees had been in it I would probably be happier, but if she was prepared to black-up that would do, but she just turned over and went to sleep, possibly because she'd have had a job getting hold of some burnt cork at eleven-o-clock at night.

****

October 22 2007. *FAT CHILDREN.*

At the age of sixty six years and seven months I have just written only my second letter to a newspaper. (My first was to Uncle Ben of the High Peak Reporter when I was ten, complaining to him that my entry in his 'What I did on my holidays' competition was far better than the entry that won. It was totally disregarded, and is probably the reason I haven't written to a newspaper since.)

The reason for abandoning my letters-to-the-editor stand was a newspaper article about Walkers Crisps. I wrote thus: -

'I read that in addition to encouraging Gary Mogadon to make those puerile TV commercials (as if we didn't see enough of him already on Match of the Day and other programmes that the BBC for some unknown reason thing he's good enough to present), that Walkers are to re-launch their 'Free Books For Schools Programme'. 'Since the scheme was launched in 1999 it has provided more than 6 million free books to schools across the country', we were proudly informed by a Walkers spokesman.

Nothing of course is free, and in this case free means that Walkers will provide one book per one school for every five hundred tokens saved from their crisps packets. I hope one of the books is called 'How To Lose Lots Of Excess Blubber' and another 'What To Do When People Start To Call You Fatty', because there are surely going to be lots of grossly overweight children around if they have to munch their way through five hundred packets of crisps every time they need a new schoolbook.

Walkers of course are not the only food company who bribe schoolchildren to eat their products in exchange for educational materials. Cadburys are another, with their internet-based 'Cadburys Learning Zone', which offers, and I quote, 'exciting and challenging materials for both school and home learning with online and download activities, fascinating facts and illustrations'. This must be the first ever programme that teaches children all about chocolate whilst at the same time teaching them how to add, subtract, multiply and divide, thus enabling them to calculate how many teeth they've lost due to eating the chocolate they've learned all about.

Cadburys also operate a scheme similar to that of Walkers and will benevolently stump up for sports equipment for schools in return for tokens collected from their range of confectionary. This of course encourages children to eat even more chocolate than they are already eating, and having eaten it presumably to take part in sports such as Five Ton-a-Side Football and The 100 Metres Very Low Hurdles Because If They Were Any Higher The Kids Wouldn't Be Able to Jump Over Them Because They Are So Grossly Overweight, Better Make That Just Fifty Metres Then, these being the only sort of sports activities their bloated frames will allow them to participate in.

Naturally our old friends McDonalds have been into this sort of thing for years. In fact in yesterday's paper there was a photograph of Newcastle and England footballer Kieran Dyer passing on tips to a clutch of schoolboy footballers who were wearing training bibs with a large McDonalds logo plastered on the front. Presumably Kieran Dyer himself eats McDonalds, and following his woeful performance in his team's thrashing by Manchester United last Saturday you would have thought that both he and McDonalds would want to keep quiet about it, but no, footballers along with food companies were seemingly on the front row when brass necks were handed out.

Now it doesn't take much of a brain to work out that the consumption of Big Macs and playing football are about as compatible as the eating of meat & potato pies and playing football, which is about as compatible as a tankful of petrol and two pounds of sugar; indeed in a fair world along with shouts from the terraces of 'You fat bastard, you ate all the pies' there would be at least an equal number of shouts of 'You fat bastard, you ate all the Big Macs'.

I must confess to not knowing the full details of what exactly McDonalds offer up in the way of freebies to children in order to coerce them to eat Big Macs but if it's anything less than a three weeks all expenses paid trip to Disneyland for each Big Mac eaten the children are being had.

McDonalds would no doubt argue, as would Walkers, that their products, in addition to being tasty, are nutritious and a source of energy. Well crisps are not too vile, as far as the plain variety goes, vileness kicking in with a vengeance when 'flavours' are added, but to defend Big Macs because they are a source of energy is like defending Saddam Hussein because he found lots of work for torturers.

Walkers, Cadburys and McDonalds are just three of the many food companies who induce children, and through them their teachers and parents, to consume their products. I don't know whether they do it for altruistic reasons, whether

84

they do it to salve their guilty consciences for encouraging children to eat junk food, or whether it's just pure greed, but if I had to put a bet on it my money would be on pure greed.'
Yours etc
Terry Ravenscroft

And guess what? They printed it. Well some of it. Edited down to about a third of it. And so highly sanitised as to make it hardly worth the bother. They even cut out the bit about Gary Mogadon. The editor is probably a descendant of Uncle Ben. I have written my last letter to a newspaper. Definitely.

****

October 30 2007. *HORSESHIT.*

In the long ago people needing to get from one place to another by the quickest means possible would go by horse. Then the motor car was invented, rendering the horse redundant as a mode of transport. Not only was the motor car quicker and a far more comfortable ride whilst travelling the country's highways and byways but it had the added benefit of not shitting on them whilst it was doing so. This happened over a century ago yet people today still feel the need to ride their horses on our roads and their horses still feel the need to shit on them.

Living in a small town with open countryside all around has a lot going for it. One of the things not going for it is having horses shit on the street where you live. There are upwards of fifty horses grazing in the fields surrounding the small housing estate on which I live. Every day at least four or five of these horses are saddled up by their owners and ridden down my street. At weekends *all* the horses are saddled up and ridden down my street. All of them shit in my street. And there the shit lies, in a big heap. Until such time as a car drives over it and bonds it to the road in a bigger, flatter, heap. And there it stays, until the rain eventually washes it away. One day I counted fifty eight heaps, some newly dumped and still steaming, some by now flattened, in the hundred yards length of my street. The situation is getting so bad that a week or so ago I sent a letter to the council suggesting they alter the name of my street from Lingland Road to Shit View. They replied that they have noted my comments and it would be discussed at the next council meeting. Yes, I'll bet it will be.

Sometimes the people who own the horses don't ride them down the street. They put the horses in the back of a van and drive the van down the street. Unbelievable. Someone invents the motor vehicle so people no longer have to ride a horse to get from A to B then the people put their horses in a van and drive it from A to B. At about ten miles - an-hour. And you drive behind it at ten miles an hour. Seething. But at least the horse isn't shitting in the road. It's shitting in the van. And you can smell it. Until such time as the van turns off, about twenty miles up the road. If you're lucky.

From reading the above it might be construed that I don't like horses. Wrong. I don't mind horses at all; especially when one of them has won me a few quid at Haydock Park. It's their shit I don't like, especially when it's in the road outside my house.

Nowadays when responsible dog owners walk their dogs they carry a poop scoop and a plastic bag and when their dog defecates they put the offending turd in the plastic bag and take it home with them. There is no reason on earth why horse owners shouldn't do the same. They would probably need a couple of bags, granted, and the filled bags would be quite heavy, but so what, they could hang them either side of their horse like saddlebags. I am seriously thinking of starting a national campaign to implement this idea. So if sometime in the future you see a horse walking along with a bag of shit slung either side of it you'll have me to thank for it.

****

November 2 2007. *GOING FOR PETROL.*

The phone rang. It was The Trouble.

"There's a light on in the car," she cooed.

"What sort of light?

"On the dashboard thingy."

"Describe it."

"Well it's just a light."

"What colour is it?"

"Do you remember those curtains we used to have in the spare bedroom? A sort of burnt orange?"

Is she joking? Probably not. "When this light came on, was there a pinging sound?"

"Er...I think so."

"You need to put some petrol in."

"How do you do that?"

It must be at least twenty years since I taught The Trouble how to drive - after insisting of course that she first had ten lessons from a qualified instructor - I'm a supportive husband, not a fool. One day when she was reasonably proficient, i.e. when people had taken to the streets again and she had mastered the nine point turn - I asked her to take the next turn on the left and pull up. She did. She looked around her and said, non-plussed, "We're in a garage."

I corrected her. "A filling station."

"Why?"

"Your next lesson. It's called 'Going for Petrol'."

I had her get out of the car and showed her how to unlock the petrol cap and use the petrol pump. I stopped when I'd put in a couple of gallons. Then I had her do the same, going through the complete routine. Three times. Satisfied that she now knew how to put petrol in the car I took her to the kiosk to show her how to pay for it. Sorted. Or so I imagined.

From that day to this I don't think she's put petrol in our car more than half-a-dozen times, and not at all in our present car, which we've had for about eighteen months. Which had prompted her question as to how to go about putting petrol in it. On more than one occasion I've seen her get in the car, switch on, notice that the needle on the fuel gauge was getting dangerously near to the red zone, and get out and either walk or take a bus to where she was going. This time she must have failed to take that precaution.

The tone of my voice was deliberately long-suffering so as to register my disapproval. Water off a duck's back I know, but you have to make an effort. "Go to the nearest garage."

"Where's that?"

"Where are you now?" She told me. "Make for Tesco's."

"Do they sell petrol?" There was real surprise in her voice. "I've never noticed when I've been there shopping."

"It's not on the shelves next to the cereals and tins of soup, it's at a separate building with a giant sign on it that says 'Petrol' - you'll see about eight things outside it that look like one-armed monsters out of Doctor Who; they're called petrol pumps."

"There's no need to be sarcastic."

"There is every need to be sarcastic."

She arrived home about an hour later, not a happy bunny. "I didn't know it cost as much as that," she complained.

"Well why would you?"

"Ninety eight pence a litre!"

"Right. How much did you put in?"

"Well a litre of course. Oh by the way, that light came on again_on the way home."

****

November 17 2007. *MISTEAK*.

The advert in the paper read -
You could urn up to £20 an hour working form home after Chapterhouse proofreeding and editing coarse.

Co-respondence courses and seminars. Fifteen ears of publishing training. Exerpt personal tutors.Advice on getting wok.

Mark he errors nad send this ad to us with your name and a dress and we'll send you our free prospectus. If your two bussy a phone call will do. 0800 3328 8396

Save up to £35 for early booking

www.chapterhousepublishing.com, 16 Magdalen Road, Exeter, EX2 45Y

I marked the errors 'MISTEAK', 'cuold', 'urn', 'form', 'ears', 'exerpt', 'he', 'a dress', 'your' and 'bussy'. I missed the spelling mistakes 'coarse, 'nad', 'proofreeding' and 'Co-respondence'. I also marked as errors the correctly spelled words 'publishing' and 'prospectus'. I sent the ad off to Chapterhouse and a few days later I received their reply, which I reprint below.

Dear Mr Ravenscroft

Welcome from all at Chapterhouse! We offer - a choice of course unrivalled **personal tuition** a track record of **success** full assessment of **all courses** a guide to finding **work** After a Chapterhouse course you could be set for a full or part-time career earning **up to £20 an hour** from home. Please read our **Brochure** and **Book of Success** We would love to have you as a student! With best wishes

Daisy Crowther, Course Director

And *that's* after returning their form with six glaring errors! **Christ** knows what they'd have **offered me** if I'd got everything right, a **directorship** a least I would have thought.

I wrote back to Daisy Crowther and told her to go fcuk herself.

****

December 29 2007. *GOOSE.*

I answered the door to Atkins. He was carrying what looked to be a coil of washing line. "What's the rope for?" I said, in a state of suspicion, which isn't a bad state to be in when dealing with Atkins.

"Didn't you once mention you used to be in the Boy Scouts?" he said, ignoring my query about the rope. It didn't take me long to find out. "Can you do a noose?" he asked, stepping inside.

Alarm bells rang. Atkins has been having an ongoing battle of wills with the paperboy, who persists in leaving the majority of his Daily Mail on the outside side of his letter box where it gets wet through if it's raining when the paper is delivered. Personally I think giving the Daily Mail a thorough dousing can only improve it but Atkins says the he likes it for the cartoons.

"You're not going to hang the paperboy, are you?" I said. "You've only got to tip him at Christmas like everybody else and he'd push your paper all the way through."

"I've never tipped in my life and I don't intend starting now," said Atkins. "It's against my religion. Anyway I'm not going to hang the paperboy, it's for the wife."

"You're going to hang Meg?"

Atkins looked at me impatiently. "I'm not going to hang anybody. She wants a goose for our New Year's Day dinner."

It transpired that Mrs Atkins had been very disappointed with the turkey they'd had for Christmas Day lunch and wasn't about to risk another disappointment. Atkins had been charged with providing a goose.

"That still doesn't explain why you want a noose," I said.

91

Atkins snorted. "Have you seen the price of them? If she thinks I'm forking out fifty quid for a goose she can think again. No, there's a flock of Canada geese on the canal, must be a hundred of them. I'm going to bag one. Lasso one. Make it wish it had never left Canada. When you've made me a noose."

What Atkins had in mind was a bit ambitious, even for Atkins. "You're going to lasso one of the Canada geese on the canal?"

"Well why not?"

"Well for one thing they're protected."

"What, you mean they were shin pads or something? Give over. Anyway I'm having one, protected or not, they won't miss one." He proffered the rope. "So if you'd be good enough to do the honours?"

I took the rope off him. "It isn't a noose you want," I said, "It's a slip knot. You want a lariat, like cowboys use."

"That's it, a lariat. Make me a lariat."

"You can use a lariat?"

"We won't be able to miss. They're all together in a big flock just sat there paddling around, the noose bit is bound to go over the neck of one of them. Then all we have to do is drag it out."

Normally when Atkins says 'we', automatically incorporating me into one of his wilder schemes, I demur, or at the very least take some time to consider what I might be getting myself into. Not this time. Atkins lassoing a goose was not a sight I wanted to miss. Geese, especially large Canada geese, are very strong birds, and once Atkins tightened the lasso round the neck of one of them it would be a racing certainty it would be the goose dragging Atkins into the canal rather than Atkins dragging the goose out of it.

After I'd made the lariat and Atkins had tried a few practice throws at our garden gnome - which he managed to lasso once out of twelve attempts, and it wasn't moving about like a Canada goose would be - we set off for the canal, Atkins claiming that he would have had much more success with the gnome had there been as many of them, and as closely bunched together, as there were of Canada geese.

We arrived at the canal. The geese were only yards away. Atkins was right, it would be more difficult to miss them than lasso one. He commenced to prove this by lassoing one at the first attempt. With a smirk and a cry of 'Yahooo' that would have done credit to Hopalong Cassidy or a demented line dancer he pulled the lariat tight. Then a strange thing happened. As I've already said, I expected the goose to pull Atkins into the canal. Not a bit of it. Instead, it just sort of stood up in the water, rather like a horse rearing up on its hind legs, then flew straight at us at about a hundred miles an hour.

"Shit a brick!" yelled Atkins.

I didn't say anything. Speechless people can't. I just turned, flew across the towpath and leapt over the stone wall into a farmer's field. Just before leaping I turned to see the goose batting Atkins round the head with its huge wings, Atkins trying manfully but unsuccessfully both to shield himself with his arms and fight off the beast at the same time.

I recovered my powers of speech just enough to shout "Let go of the rope you bloody fool!" before landing on the other side of the wall and haring off down the field fifty yards or so before slithering to a halt and chancing a look back. A second or so later Atkins's head, dishevelled and sorry-looking, appeared above the wall, his hands pulling small feathers from his hair.

"You got rid of it then?" I called.

"It flew off," he answered, then added, sorrowfully, "And so did all its mates."

I made my way back to him. "What are you going to do then?" I asked.

"She'll have to settle for duck," he said. "Anyway I prefer duck."

****

February 22 2008. *AIR MAIL.*

About ten years ago, whilst flying home from a holiday in Lanzarote, I was served the most revolting lasagne I have ever tasted. It was so bad that if I'd had to choose between eating it and death I would not be here now, death being the preferred option. The following day I wrote about it to Air 2000, the airline company concerned. I presumed that they would have fielded many complaints about their lasagne and so in order to ring the changes I wrote in praise of it. This is the letter: -

Dear Air 2000

I recently had the pleasure of flying for the very first time. I've always been afraid to up until now, but I finally plucked up courage. I am certainly glad that I did, and for two reasons. One, it wasn't half so bad an experience as I had imagined it would be, and two, I had my first meal on an aeroplane. Why all the jokes about airline food? The fare we

94

were served by Air 2000 on our flights down to Lanzarote and back were quite excellent, and I speak as a man who knows good food, eating as I do at least five ready-to-heat-up-in-the-microwave or boil-in-the-bag meals a week. Both the turkey and stuffing going down and the lasagne coming back were quite mouth-watering. Nor could I fault the starters and desserts, although it must be said that the couple seated next to me detected a 'soapy' taste in the trifle, although if you ask me it was their imagination, because it certainly tasted all right to me.

Is it possible to buy your meals? If so, could you please reply, with details of any other meals you do, your price list, and any discounts you allow for quantity.

Yours sincerely

T Ravenscroft (Mr)

Air 2000 replied to my letter much as I suspected they might, pleased to note that I enjoyed the lasagne but regretting that the meals they served onboard were not available for re-sale. The matter would have ended there if they hadn't then added the following sentence, which was, and I quote, '*Nevertheless, we would be very pleased to welcome you on board again in the near future, to sample the refreshments within our service once again*'.

Now I could have taken this two ways; one, that they would be very happy if I chose to fly with them again (which is what they had meant). And two, that they were offering me a free trip in order that I could have another one of their delightful meals (which is what I chose to believe they had meant).

After three more exchanges of correspondence, by which time I had decided I'd led Air 2000 up the garden path for long enough, it occurred to me that two other incidents worthy of complaint had occurred during my flight; one was that from my window seat I couldn't see the television set located in the central aisle without leaning over to a degree well in excess of the lean on the Tower of Pisa if I were to view the screen in full; the other was that I was ripped off to the tune of about twenty-five per cent when changing my Spanish pesetas back into sterling. I saw a book looming.

Rather than write to Air 2000 again, who no doubt would have had enough of me by then, I complained to two other airline companies. Their replies and the subsequent correspondence encouraged me to write to other airline companies, but this time with complaints I had made up. There are only so many things one can complain about, even to airlines, so I also wrote to some of them in praise of their service and to others with requests for advice. A book, which I called Dear Air 2000 in honour of the first of my letters, was the result.

Dear Air 2000 must have set a world record for being turned down because over the course of the next five years there wasn't one publisher I sent it to who didn't reject it. Not all of them turned it down out of hand; in fact some were quite complimentary about it. One went as far as to say "This is the funniest book I've read in ages. If you were Ben Elton I'd publish it tomorrow. But who is Terry Ravenscroft?' (Publishers, along with most people I would guess, don't read the credits at the end of television programmes or he might have known.)

That's the way things are in the book publishing industry I'm afraid, even more so now, in 2008 than it was back then.

Publishers nowadays aren't selling books, they're selling names. There is no doubt that if Victoria Beckham were to announce she was planning a book called 'The Thoughts of Victoria Beckham' publishers would be falling over their cheque books in the rush to offer her a million pounds advance. That 'The Thoughts of Victoria Beckham' would be an exceptionally thin book containing just one chapter entitled 'Shopping' wouldn't affect their interest in it in the slightest. 'Kylie Minogue's Road Kill Recipes' would be welcomed with open arms.

Eventually I gave up the ghost and published Dear Air 2000 myself, a relatively inexpensive and easy matter nowadays with 'print on demand' technology. But publishing it, I was soon to discover, was the easy part. Trying to sell it was a different matter entirely. Amazon stocked it (they stock nearly all published books, bless them), but W H Smiths, Waterstone's and Borders didn't want to know, possibly applying the 'Ben Elton who is Terry Ravenscroft' principle'.

To promote the book I sent a copy to eighty commercial radio presenters, asking them to read it and if they liked it to give it a mention on their show. I don't know how many did but seven of them liked it enough to give me an on air interview. The book started to sell on Amazon.

I was convinced it would sell in bookshops too, and because of its subject matter especially so in airline bookshops, if only I could get it on their shelves. I decided to find out for definite. I was going on holiday and arrived at Manchester Airport an hour earlier than I needed to. As soon as I'd checked in I discreetly placed five copies of Dear Air 2000 in a prominent position on the shelves of W H Smith's air side bookshop and stood by to watch what would happen.

After forty five minutes five people had picked up the book and glanced through it. Four of them had gone to the counter to buy it. They weren't able to of course because the bar code wouldn't scan. The first time this happened the assistant called for the manager. Heads were scratched and apologies made to the prospective customer. Telephone calls, presumably to head office, were made. In the meantime a second customer arrived at the counter wanting to buy the book. Money did eventually change hands and two satisfied customers departed with copies of Dear Air 2000. How the sales were accounted for I have no idea, nor did I care; I had made my point.

It had been my intention to get in touch with W H Smith on my return from holiday to report what had happened, but on arriving home a letter was waiting for me. It was from publisher Michael O'Mara Books, from Michael O'Mara himself no less. He had come by a copy of Air 2000, he wanted to publish it himself, he would give me a substantial advance, was I interested? Does the Pope shit on Catholics? Dear Air 2000 was re-published as 'Air Mail' and sold in bookshops with a gratifying degree of success.

I hadn't the heart to tell Michael O'Mara that Michael O'Mara Books had turned the book down when I had offered it to them two years ago, along with all those other short-sighted publishers.

****

March 16 2008. *AN AMBITION FULFILLED.*

My front drive is fourteen feet wide, exactly the same width as the local canal at its narrowest point. Using the edges of my drive as a guide I had chalked lines across the pavement to represent the canal. Now I walked along the footpath for some twenty yards, turned, ran back at full pelt, hit the first chalk line, leapt, and landed about a foot beyond the second chalk line. I retraced my steps and did the same again, putting a little more effort into it. This time I cleared the second chalk line by a good two feet, a leap in excess of sixteen feet. I then jumped across the lines in the reverse direction, with the same result. It was then that Atkins happened by, on his way to buy his morning newspaper.

Don't tell me," he said "you asked The Trouble to dress up as a schoolgirl and she told you to take a running jump."

He wasn't far off the mark as far as The Trouble telling me to take a running jump was concerned as I was in the doghouse for telling her Feng Shui instructor to clear off when he called round to rearrange our furniture again and she wasn't in. "I'm going to jump the canal," I said.

Atkins was impressed. "Really?"

"Really."

"When are you doing it? I want to be there," he said eagerly, no doubt hoping the same disaster that befell him when he went goose-hunting would befall me. "I'll act as your second. Carry a dry set of clothing for you and a towel."

"There'll be no need for that," I said, "It's a done job."

Jumping over the canal at its narrowest point (known to everyone as 'the narrow hole') has long been an ambition of mine. In fact I've wanted to do it since I was a boy. During my schooldays I was a fair athlete, I always won the hundred yards in my age group at the school sports and the long jump with it, and could jump over twenty feet when I was fifteen. Jumping over the canal should have presented no problem at all. But I never did it. I've jumped in it. And over the years

I've walked by it, fell in it, paddled in it, peed in it (both while I was paddling in it and from the towpath), fished in it, skimmed stones on it, skated on it and made love on the grass verge which separates it from its towpath. But never jumped it.

Lots of my schoolmates jumped it, nearly all of them, including boys who couldn't jump anywhere near as far as I could. Even two girls had jumped it. The only casualty had been Bucktooth Dawson, and even he cleared it, the casualty being when his impetus on landing kept him running and he ran into a tree and knocked his front teeth out. (Disappointingly for him people still called him bucktooth. He pointed out that he now hadn't any teeth and therefore his nickname should now be Buck, which he would have enjoyed as he liked cowboy pictures, but nobody took any notice of course, children being children.

I never did jump it. Something always stopped me. The fear of falling in and making a fool of myself I suppose, even though I knew I was more than capable of clearing it. But I never forgot it, and many times since I've sworn that one day I *would* do it. So today, at the age of sixty-seven, after satisfying myself that I could still easily jump the fourteen feet required, I set out to do it. I allowed Atkins to accompany me but spurned his offer of videoing the occasion for a potential 'You've Been Framed' clip.

I didn't mess about when we got there, I just backed away from the water's edge as far as I could, ran, then soared over the canal like a gazelle, landing on the other side with a good three feet to spare. Atkins was most impressed, and applauded, but failed to hide his disappointment.

When my schoolmates had jumped it all those years ago it wasn't really a proposition to jump back as the land on the opposite side of the canal sloped away quite steeply and was composed largely of grass tussocks and the occasional cowpat, making a return jump much more difficult. So having leapt the canal the way back was down through the fields and return via the footbridge some hundred yards or so down the canal. Which is what I intended to do. Except that I now found out I couldn't. In front of me was not an open field but a housing estate, and my way was blocked by a ten feet high back garden fence.

I pointed out my predicament to Atkins. "Just climb over the fence," he called.

"You must be joking."

"You'll have to jump back over the canal then."

"You must be joking."

"You'll have to stay there and starve to death then."

This is where my National Service survival training came in. "There are some planks in my garage. Nip back and get a couple of them to make a bridge over the canal."

Atkins nodded. "It's as good as done." Good old Atkins, I thought, a friend in need.

Four hours I waited there. He eventually returned just before dark, two planks over his shoulder. Naturally by then I was fuming. "What the bloody hell kept you?" I demanded.

"Sorry. Your garage was locked and when I asked The Trouble for the key she wanted to know what I wanted it for and I told her and she told me to clear off and to tell you what it feels like to be told to clear off like you told her Feng Shui instructor to clear off. Anyway I haven't got any planks and I don't know anybody who has so I had to buy a couple, you owe me fifteen quid."

No, I didn't fall into the canal when I crossed the planks, thank you for asking, although by then I couldn't have cared less if I had.

****

May 2 2008. *SWIMMING LESSONS.*

A few weeks ago The Trouble indicated something in the freebie newspaper that had caught her eye. "Have you read this?" she said. "It's just what you need."

I looked to where she was pointing. "Incontinence pants? My trouble is not being able to pee, not peeing too much."

"Not that! Underneath." She read it out. Apparently the local leisure centre would be holding free swimming lessons specially designed for Oldies. She suggested again that I might take advantage of the offer.

"Why?" I asked. "I've got by for the best part of seventy years without knowing how to swim, I'm sure I can manage a bit longer."

"People who do as much walking along the canal as you do should be able to swim," The Trouble argued. "What if you were to fall in?"

"I've managed to avoid falling in up until now."

"You had a narrow escape not long back And you're getting older . What if you had a dizzy spell?

"I don't have dizzy spells."

"Not yet. But you might start getting them."

I thought about it. Maybe there was something in what The Trouble was saying. Maybe I might start getting the odd dizzy spell now I'm well into my sixties, I've heard of other people my age who have started having them. I decided to go for it, as they say nowadays, and a couple of weeks later found me presenting myself at the swimming pool at the appointed hour of 9 a.m. Apparently there would be twenty lessons in all, one every Monday morning. I would very soon be Ian Thorpe.

There were twelve would-be swimmers in total, all male, the powers-that-be having deemed that any prospective Oldie women swimmers would be accommodated in another session, possibly on the grounds that the swimming lessons would go more swimmingly if any scope for hanky-panky had been eliminated.

Of the twelve of us one man has only one leg, one must weigh thirty stones if he weighs an ounce, one is a dwarf, and one is a hunchback. The other eight of us could be classified as normal, although two of them can't be a day under ninety and another has a glass eye, which strictly speaking is not completely normal, but a lot more normal than the four I've mentioned. Lined up we must have looked like we were auditioning for Star Wars 7, The Return of the Grotesques.

I had grave doubts that when the fat one entered the pool he would displace such a volume of water that we'd all be swimming in the rafters but I kept my thoughts to myself, at least for the time being. But watch this space.

"Have you all brought along your birth certificates?" the swimming instructor now asked.

Well I hadn't and nor had any of the others judging from their reactions.

"I didn't know I was supposed to," said the man with the glass eye.

The instructor gave a long-suffering sigh. "How am I supposed to know if you are entitled to free swimming lessons if you haven't brought along you birth certificate?"

"How am I supposed to know you're a swimming instructor?" the man with the glass eye, sharp as a tack, shot back at her,

"Because I've got a whistle round my neck," she said.

I almost chipped in with "You could be the referee for the five-a-side football in the gym and you've turned up at the wrong venue," but held back, mindful that she was a woman who would very soon have my life in her hands.

"I sincerely hope you've all brought swimwear?" the instructor asked, our inability to have brought our birth certificates obviously prompting the enquiry. "If not you can hire one," she added.

One of we normal ones raised a hand and said, a little embarrassed, "Where can you hire them?"

The hunchback, demonstrating a ready sense of humour despite his affliction, said, "There's a little press stud on the waistband, you just push it and up they go." I'd have been proud of that one myself.

After we'd all got kitted out the lesson began. First we had to lie flat on our bellies and do the breast stroke, as demonstrated by the lady instructor. This involved moving our arms and legs, or in the case of the one-legged man his arms and leg, in a sort of frog-like motion. After a minute or so the one-legged man asked, reasonably enough, if, once he was in the pool, his being minus a leg might cause him to go round in circles rather than in a straight line. The instructor said she hadn't come across this potential problem before but that they would "cross that bridge when they came to it."

A bridge that needed to be crossed immediately, as we'd already come to it, was that the fat man, balancing somewhat precariously on his belly, kept toppling over every time he made more than the smallest frog-like motion with his arms

104

and legs, and on a couple of occasions would have squashed the man with the glass eye and maybe caused his glass eye to pop out if the latter hadn't had the good sense to fling himself out of the fat man's path. The instructor solved this hitch in proceedings by moving the fat man over against a wall, which stopped him toppling over on that side, and by shoring up his other side with the aid two medicine balls borrowed from the fitness centre.

The hunchback, demonstrating his sense of humour again, said he was thankful we weren't doing the back stroke or he'd be in the same boat and would also require shoring up. His mention of boats got me thinking that if you wished to propel yourself through water then a boat would be a far easier and safer way of achieving this rather than by swimming; certainly a less tiring way, as after about five minutes of lying on my belly and moving my arms and legs in frog-like motions I was absolutely knackered. I mentioned this to the instructor who said that once we were in the pool it wouldn't be so tiring due to the buoyancy of the water. Fortunately we were then asked to get in the pool to test out this theory.

At this point the fat man excused himself as he 'wanted the lavatory'. I hazarded a guess that it would be doubtful if the lavatory would feel the same way about him once he'd deposited his thirty stones on it.

There were stone steps down into the pool, which is three feet six inches deep at the shallow end. When we walked down the steps the dwarf, at three feet at the most, disappeared completely under water before bobbing to the surface again and splashing for dear life in a furious mixture of the front crawl, backstroke, butterfly and dog paddle. The instructor, obviously never having had to instruct a three foot dwarf trying to stand up in a three feet six deep pool before, told him to get out while she had a think about it.

The fat fuck returned from the gents - the reader will see why I have relegated him from a fat man to a fat fuck in a moment - and eschewing the steps, and quite without warning, jumped into the pool. A wave of tsunami proportions headed for me at about two hundred miles-an-hour, completely engulfing me and filling my eyes with the heavily-chlorinated water. Minutes later my eyes were red raw from a combination of the effects of the chlorine and from rubbing them, and several hours later I still looked like something out of a Hammer horror film. The Trouble couldn't look at me without her eyes watering.

The following Monday, more than a little dubious about continuing after what had happened the week before, but having taken the precaution of equipping myself with a pair of goggles should the fat fuck Mr Liddiard take it upon himself to jump in the pool again, I went for my second lesson. I was glad I did because it went a lot more successfully for me than had the first. The same can't be said for one of my fellow learner swimmers, the dwarf, Mr Leeson, for reasons which I will now disclose.

One of the teaching techniques employed by the swimming instructor, Miss Hobday, is to have the learner swimmers stand in the shallow end of the pool, squat down a little so that their shoulders are level with the top of the water, and practice the arm movements of the breast stroke whilst walking along the bottom. This, she assured us, would give us the feel of actually swimming in addition to building up our confidence.

This exercise is fine for people of normal height, but as I have already mentioned the shallow end of the pool is three feet deep six and Mr Leeson is only three feet tall, a discrepancy of six inches on the part of Mr Leeson. Last week when Mr Leeson got in the pool and promptly disappeared underwater he quickly got out again before he drowned. He obviously didn't want the same thing to happen again so when Miss Hobday - who had more than likely instructed dozens of other would-be swimmers since our session last week and had probably forgotten all about Mr Leeson's problem - asked us all to get into the pool, Mr Leeson refused point blank, and went on to tell Miss Hobday his reason for refusing, i.e. that if he did he may never live to tell the tale.

Miss Hobday had a think about it but from her bemused expression clearly a solution to the problem was beyond her. She told us to practise the arm movements of the breast stroke on dry land and disappeared for about ten minutes. When she returned, obviously having taken counsel from a higher authority, she told Mr Leeson that to overcome the problem he would be transferred to the ten-year-olds' swimming classes, where the pupils would be the same size as he was. She added that unfortunately, unlike the Oldie lessons, the lessons wouldn't be free and would have to be paid for by Mr Leeson, but it was the best she could do under the circumstances.

Mr Leeson hit the roof. Or as near to the roof as it's possible for a dwarf to hit it. "Are you joking?" he protested. "If you think you're putting me in with a load of ten-year-old kids and expecting me to pay for the privilege you've got another think coming. People will accuse me of being a bloody paedophile!"

"Yes, I've already had to stop being a Santa Claus because of that," said one of the normal men, Mr Littlewood, although without bothering to enlarge on his statement.

"And anyway," said Mr Pargeter, the man with the glass eye, "How do you manage to teach children? If they're the same height as Mr Leeson how come they don't disappear under the water?"

A good point, and one I hadn't thought of myself.

"Yes, if the water goes over Mr Leeson's head it'll go over a child's head as well," said the hunchback, Mr Gearing, adding his three-pennyworth.

Miss Hobday had the answer however. "We use a different teaching system for children," she said primly.

"Well then use your usual system for us and the children's system for Mr Leeson," said Mr Pargeter.

Rather reluctantly, and against her better judgement it seemed to me, Miss Hobday agreed to do this, starting the following week.

One week on we found that the system employed by the local leisure centre to teach ten-year-olds is to first kit out him or her with inflatable arm and leg bands. Having been made buoyant little Brad or little Angelina is then fitted with a shoulder harness attached to a long length of rope. The child then gets in the water and whilst simulating the arm and leg movements of the breast stroke is gently towed across the width of the pool by the instructor. The idea is that over a period of time the child will become less and less dependent on the arm and leg bands, the harness and tow rope, and will eventually be able to swim unaided.

This system was now being employed by Miss Hobday to instruct Mr Leeson. Naturally when she is towing Mr Leeson to and fro across the pool she can't be instructing the eleven non-dwarfs in her class, who are left to their own devices. Miss Hobday apologised in advance for this inconvenience but said there was nothing she could do about it, that another instructor couldn't be spared, they didn't grow on trees, and that she had been told by her superiors to devote half her time to teaching Mr Leeson to swim by the ten-year-olds' method, and the other half to teaching the rest of us to swim by the normal method.

One of the normal men using the normal method men, Mr Hall, said that this was patently unfair as there were eleven non-dwarfs in our group and only one dwarf, and that to be fair our hour's instruction should be split up in the ratio 11.1, eleven parts going to the normals and one part to the dwarf. Mr Leeson said this would mean that it would give him only five minutes instruction time per session while the rest of us would have fifty five minutes, which was not only clearly unfair but also discrimination against dwarfs.

Before Miss Hobday could make a ruling on this the fat fuck Mr Liddiard complicated matters further by saying that he too wanted to be treated like a ten-year-old and be kitted out with arm and leg bands and towed across the pool by Miss Hobday.

There is a little history with Mr Liddiard and Miss Hobday, inasmuch as just before the session was about to begin Mr Liddiard had taken it upon himself to jump into the pool again, despite having been warned not to do so after what had happened to me during our first lesson. Fortunately no one was in the pool this time so nobody was in danger of being drowned, but the resultant splash drenched Miss Hobday, who was standing by the poolside, immediately transforming her neatly-ironed white top and shorts into saturated and see-through top and shorts, and her neatly coiffed hair into a bedraggled mess. This could well explain what she then said to Mr Liddiard, after he had asked to be treated like a ten-year-old and be kitted out with arm and leg bands and towed across the pool, which was, and I quote, "If I can get hold of four Goodyear blimps for your arm and leg bands and a ten ton lorry to tow you across the pool I will do that; in the meantime you'll have to stay with the others."

Five of us, including me, applauded her. The man with the glass eye, Mr Pargeter, and the man with the hunchback, Mr Gearing, laughed out loud, but then both had axes to grind, Mr Liddiard having previously referred to them, within their hearing, as Quasimodo and Cyclops.

Mr Liddiard, by now red-faced and fuming, stomped from the scene without a word, and that was the last we ever saw of him. Five minutes later Miss Hobday was summoned to the office. Ominously, we didn't see her again either.

The following week, about half-an-hour before I was due to set off for my next lesson, I had a phone call from the manageress of the leisure centre telling me not to bother, as following her altercation with Mr Liddiard last week Miss Hobday had been suspended on full pay until such time as the matter had been fully investigated by an independent body and a decision made as to her future. The manageress went on to inform me that they were trying to find a replacement for Miss Hobday but that she didn't hold out much hope because 'you know how things are'.

I said, "No, I don't know how things are, how are they?"

"Well it's such a long drawn out process getting a replacement," she explained, "with all the vetting we have to do in case the applicants are paedophiles or sex crimes offenders, and what with instructors coming into contact with children and vulnerable adults. It would be more than likely that Miss Hobday will be back with us by the time the vetting is completed so it just wouldn't be worth our while trying to get a replacement."

I thought about this for a moment then played what I thought was a trump card. "You do realise you're discriminating against Mr Leeson, do you?"

A slight pause. "Is he the dwarf?"

"Yes."

"No, we're not. We've managed to get the dwarf, the fat man and the gentleman with the hump back in with another group."

I went berserk. "The fat man? The bloody fat man? He's the cause of all the trouble!"

"Maybe he is," said the manageress, keeping her cool, "but that doesn't give us *carte blanche* to discriminate against him."

"And what about the rest of us?"

"What do you mean?"

"Well you're discriminating against us as well. You're discriminating against us for not being dwarves, fat men or hunchbacks."

She thought about this for a moment before saying, "Well I suppose we are in a way." But then added, a note of relief in her voice, "But you can't discriminate against people for being normal."

And she was right of course. You can't. I tried a different tack. "What about the man with the glass eye?"

"What man with what glass eye?"

"Mr Pargeter. You don't think he'll sue you for discriminating against people with only one eye when he hears about what you've done for the others?"

"Thanks for the tip off," she said, relieved. "We'll be getting in touch with him. Well goodbye."

"I've got a club foot!" I yelled , before she could hang up.

There was silence on the other end of the line for a moment, then, "A club foot?"

"Yes."

More silence, then a rustling of papers, the manageress obviously checking up on my application form. "It doesn't say anything here about you having a club foot?"

"I don't like to make a fuss about it."

More silence, then she said, "Can you make Tuesdays at 10.30?"

"I think I should be able to limp along to that," I said. "God willing."

Since then, and before joining the 10.30 Tuesday swimming class at the invitation of the manageress, I discovered, thanks to a chance meeting in Matalan with the hunchback Mr Gearing - apparently their jumpers are the only ones that will fit him - that the class in question is the female equivalent of our men's Oldies class. Evidently the leisure centre powers-that-be had decided in their wisdom to lump us all together, disregarding their previous reservations about the risk of possible hanky-panky, rather than take the risk of being sued by the hunchback Mr Gearing, the dwarf Mr Leeson, the fat pillock Mr Liddiard, the man with the glass eye Mr Pargiter, and the man with the club foot, me.

In the event I had second thoughts and didn't continue with the swimming lessons. I knew what would happen. Once the instructor had started to give Mr Leeson individual tuition by towing him across the pool Mr Liddiard would demand the same treatment. What would happen after that I don't know, except that it would be some sort of almighty shambles, but whatever it was it certainly didn't warrant my having to pretend I have a club foot.

And so my swimming career came to a premature end, even before it had ever really started. And if I fall in the canal I shall just have to take my chances; it's not all that deep anyway.

April 28 2008. *BALL PARK PRICE.*

I'd gone shopping for a new up-and-over garage door as the other one has never been quite the same since The Trouble backed into it when she was going through the menopause. Neither has The Trouble for that matter, but whether it's because of the menopause or backing into the garage door I'm not sure.

After taking the particulars of my garage door the salesman worked out a price and said, "Ball park, £210."

If there's anything guaranteed to get my goat it's the Americanisation of the English language. I treated him to a withering look, and then in my best clipped Captain Mainwaring tone said, "What was that you said?"

"It'll be £210. Ball park."

I slipped Walmington-on-Sea's finest into overdrive. "And which ball park would that be then?

"What?"

"Yankee Stadium? Shea Stadium? Candlestick Park?"

"I'm sorry?"

"They're ball parks. Or perhaps it's some other ball park to which you refer?"

A bemused shake of the head. "I'm not with you."

I came to his assistance. "I mean when you said the ball park price was £210?"

He shrugged. "I meant it's just a ball park price."

"So it's any ball park then?"

"….Well, yes. I suppose."

"So what's the normal price?"

"The normal price?"

"The price that isn't the ball park price?"

"….Well, it's the same."

"The same?"

"The same as the ball park price."

"Then why call it the ball park price?"

"….Well…..well it's just an expression, that's all."

"Well here's another expression. You know where you can stick your ball park price, along with your up-and-over garage door."

After shopping around for the rest of the morning the best price I was able to get for a new garage door was £230, so it looks like my intolerance will be costing me £20. But as this isn't a ball park price it will cheap at the price.

****

April 29 2008. *I DON'T BELIEVE IT!.*

I told The Trouble about the ball park incident yesterday and far from being on my side she just shook her head and said, "You're getting more like Victor Meldrew every day."

I didn't argue with her because she's probably right, there being little doubt that the older I have grown the more intolerant I have become. Mention of the late-lamented Victor reminded me that at the time 'One Foot in the Grave' finally put both its feet in the grave because writer of the show David Renwick had run out of ideas for more episodes I heard an opinion ventured on some TV show or other that perhaps another writer could have taken over writing of it.

This suggestion was ridiculed, the one doing the ridiculing advancing the opinion that there wasn't a writer capable of taking over from Renwick. Rubbish. I know David and I'm sure he would agree with me. I had the scenario for the first half of an episode in five minutes flat.

The scene - The Meldrew's Living Room. Victor has a streaming cold and is halfway through a large brandy and hot lemon. The phone rings. Victor answers it. The caller wants to know how much Victor wants for his elephant.

Victor: "Elephant? What are you talking about? I haven't got an elephant!"

He sits down, muttering to himself and Margaret about wrong numbers. The phone rings again. It's another caller wanting to buy Victor's elephant.

Victor: "I haven't got a bloody elephant. Anyway, what on earth do you want with an elephant?"

The caller explains that an elephant has escaped from a nearby circus winter quarters and the owners are advertising in the local newspaper, offering a £5000 reward for its safe return. The caller was hoping to buy Victor's elephant for less than this and pocket the difference. Victor puts the phone down thoughtfully. An alarm bell rings in his head. An unbelievable thought strikes him. He picks up the newspaper, turns to the small ads section.

Victor: "I don't believe it!"

Margaret: "What don't you believe now?

Victor: "That advertisement I put in the 'Lost and Found' column for my lost watch - they've only gone and got it mixed up with the advert for a lost circus elephant!"

The phone rings again. Victor picks it up, listens for a moment, shouts into it "I haven't got a bloody elephant,"

115

glares at it, leaves it off the hook and says to Margaret, "I'm going for that hot bath now, try to shake off this blasted cold."

We pick up Victor emerging from the shower. He has a towel wrapped round his waist. While he is making for the bedroom he is wrapping another towel round his head in the form of a turban. Passing the bedroom window he happens to glance through it. His jaw drops.

Victor: "I don't believe it!"

From Victor's point of view we see his back garden. There is an elephant in it. He rushes downstairs to tell Margaret. They look at the elephant through the window.

Margaret: "The escaped circus elephant!"

The elephant starts eating Victor's rhubarb.

Victor: "It...it's eating my rhubarb!"

The elephant does a dump.

Victor: "Now it's going in at one end and coming out of the other. It's manuring the bloody garden now!"

Margaret: "Well you can't fault it environmentally."

Victor: "Bugger the environment, it's taken me six weeks to force that rhubarb through."

Margaret: "It isn't taking the elephant that long."

Margaret tells Victor he must get onto the circus immediately and get someone to come for the elephant. However Victor has designs on the £5000 reward. He fears the elephant might make off before its owner arrives, so decides to take it back himself as the circus winter headquarters being only a mile up the road. He ties a rope round the elephant's neck to lead it away. It won't budge. Margaret suggests that as it's a circus elephant it might be more inclined to move if he were to get on its back and ride it.

116

Victor: "Who do you think I am, Sabu?"

Margaret: "Well you certainly look like Sabu!" (The reader will recall that Victor is still dressed in a towel round his waist and has another towel wrapped round his head like a turban.)

Victor still can't budge the elephant and eventually adopts Margaret's suggestion. Lo and behold it works and Victor, atop the elephant, sets off for the circus. A hundred yards down the road a police car stops him.

Policeman: "Who do you think you are, Sabu?"

Victor: "Don't *you* bloody start!"

The policeman smells alcohol on Victor's breath and breathalyses him. (You will also recall that quite recently Victor had a large brandy.)

Victor: "I *do* believe it - you bloody people would breathalyse someone if you suspected him of sucking a beer mat!"

The breathalyser turns green and the police take Victor to the police station....with hilarious consequences, as they say.

Piece of cake.

****

May 18 2008. *SHIT GARDEN OF THE YEAR.*

In the front garden of the house was the complete back axle assembly of a large lorry, a car wing, a supermarket trolley with the wheels missing, a pram with the wheels missing, two bike frames, a bath, half a WC, a roll of carpet, two live hens and sundry other bric-a-brac including paper, polythene packaging and dead leaves. All except for the two hens were partially submerged in what was once a lawn but now resembled elephant grass. The front door bore traces of the

117

last three colours it had been painted and had 'Piss Off' in large letters written on it in spray paint. Atkins and I approached it. Atkins knocked on it. It was answered by a man who hadn't troubled himself to put on a shirt that day, relying on just his filthy vest to impress any callers.

"Congratulations," said Atkins. "You have won the 'Shit Garden of the Year' trophy."

"For the second year running," I added, holding up the trophy, an old car tyre that Atkins had sprayed metallic gold.

"Oh it's you two twats again, is it," said the proud winner. "Why don't you fuck off and mind your own business."

"Cluck cluck," said one of the hens, as if in agreement with its master's sentiments.

"It *is* our business when your garden brings down the whole tone of the neighbourhood and wipes God knows how much value off the properties in the immediate vicinity," I said.

"One of which is mine," said Atkins meaningfully.

"There's no law says I have to keep my garden tidy," said the man. "This isn't a council house."

"Obviously, otherwise you'd have been turfed out of it years ago," I said.

"Fuck off," the man said, and slammed the door in our faces.

I threw his trophy on the pile of junk already in the garden. It increased it in volume by about one per cent and in value by about fifty per cent.

"Looks like it will have to be Plan B, Terence my boy" said Atkins.

****

118

May 25 2008. *LEG OF LAMB.*

"This leg of lamb," I said to the young girl assistant in charge of the 'reduced to clear' gun at the Co-op Late Shop. "I see it reaches its sell-by date tomorrow."

She looked at the label. "That's right. May 26."

I was making an attempt at getting a supermarket assistant to put a 'reduced to clear' sticker onto something that hadn't yet outlived its shelf life. Not wishing to be too brazen about it by asking her to reduce the price of something still some way to being out of date, I had picked on something that would soon be receiving a sticker in the normal course of events. I checked my watch. "Well it's nine forty-five p.m. now and you close at ten," I said, "So it's very unlikely that anyone will buy it now. And tomorrow you'll be putting a 'reduced to clear' sticker on it. So I was wondering, if it isn't too much trouble, if you could see your way to putting one on now?"

I was going to write 'You would have thought from her expression I had asked her to show her arse in the High Street' but it occurred to me that most girls of her age do now show a good proportion of their arse in the High Street in the normal course of events, and to show all of it wouldn't make a great deal of difference; so I will just say that she looked at me with absolute amazement. "I can't do that!" she said.

The answer I'd been expecting so I was ready for her. "I am not a rich man," I said, "as you can see from my clothes." (I had taken the trouble to dress in the oldest clothes I could find and before entering the Late Shop and had lain down and rolled over in their car park, which added to my shabby appearance.) "So lamb is a luxury for me,

119

unless it's a bit of scrag end. However it is my dear wife's birthday tomorrow and ever since we were married forty-odd years ago I have cooked for her a leg of lamb dinner with all the trimmings to celebrate the occasion. Sadly I lost my job five years ago and have been unable to find employment since. Even B&Q turned me down. Things have been a bit tight to say the least. Despite that I have always managed somehow or other to scrape together enough money to buy a leg of lamb for my wife's birthday treat. And I managed to do so again this year but this morning the gas man called and threatened to cut us off if I didn't pay an outstanding bill. I hadn't got enough to pay it without the leg of lamb money so I had to use that. Besides, if I hadn't we wouldn't have had any gas with which to cook the leg of lamb, and at least by paying the gas bill we would have heat to warm our brittle old bones in the twilight of our years, even if we were hungry."

"You could have cooked it in the microwave," the girl said, helpfully, after a pause.

"Re-possessed long since with the barbecue," I replied immediately, and added, just in case she should suggest them, "Along with the electric frying-pan and the Primas stove."

"What a shame," she said, with genuine concern.

"Yes," I agreed. I went for the jugular. "But a greater shame is that this is the last time I would ever be cooking a leg of lamb for my wife's birthday, as the doctor has given her only six weeks to live."

A tear actually ran down her cheek. She looked over her shoulder to see if anyone was looking, then quickly put a 'reduced to clear' sticker on the leg of lamb and wrote '£1' in the price column. Then, with the same eye that had moments before shed a tear, she winked at me, kissed me quickly on the cheek and was gone.

The leg of lamb was lovely. The Trouble did it with a butter, breadcrumbs, garlic and fresh rosemary crust along with roast vegetables.

****

June 19 2008. *SHIT GARDEN OF THE YEAR 2.*

Today saw the culmination of Plan B of 'Shit Garden of the Year'. The plan was put into operation two weeks ago when I phoned the owner of the aforementioned shit garden. The call was answered by the titleholder's wife.

"Hello?"

"This is the High Peak Borough Council, Mr Lloyd speaking, Public Affairs and Events," I lied. "Could I speak to your husband?"

"What for? Only he's doing his pigeons and he doesn't like to be disturbed when he's doing his pigeons."

"Well whatever he's doing to his pigeons, legal or otherwise, I can assure you it will be worth his while to tear himself away from them for a short while."

"I'll have to see what he says."

"It will probably be 'Coo'," I said, but I think she'd gone. Half a minute later the man of the house, Mr Broadhurst, came on the line. "What do you want?" This uttered in a tone as suspicious as a milk bill.

"Princess Anne, the Princess Royal, is visiting the borough two weeks hence and Her Royal Highness has expressed the desire to visit a typical house within the borough. We held a raffle and your house came out of the hat."

There was silence on the other end of the phone.

"Hello? Are you still there?"

I heard the woman's voice in the background. "What is it? What's the matter, Norman?"

"Two fucking princesses are going to visit our house!"

I saw where Norman had gone wrong and put him right. "No, it's only the one princess. Princess Anne and The Princess Royal are the same person. And I don't think she'll be doing any fucking either, this isn't Fergie we're talking about here."

"No." A pause, then, "What do we have to do?"

"Not a thing. Her Royal Highness has expressed a wish that you shouldn't go to any special trouble. I believe it's usual to offer her a cup of tea. And maybe a cucumber sandwich."

"Get a cucumber next time you go to the Co-op, Deidre."

"And perhaps she could partake of the refreshments in the front garden if the weather is clement?"

"Right. In the front garden."

"Now you're not to go to any special trouble," I warned. "The Princess is quite adamant on that point and wouldn't like it."

"No. No special trouble."

"And a word to the wise. Keep it to yourself. We don't want the neighbours gawking."

"Right."

"I'll confirm the arrangements to you by letter."

Atkins and I went round to the Broadhurst's house at the appointed hour this afternoon. The garden, of course, was immaculate; vultures working round the clock couldn't have stripped it off the sundry detritus more efficiently. To complement it the exterior of the house had been cleaned up and newly painted, the windows sparkled. Red, white and blue bunting decorated the façade. It looked a real picture. A small crowd, maybe about a hundred and fifty, many with small union jack flags, had gathered. The owner of the 'Shit Garden of the Year' and his wife were at the open doorway, all smiles, he wearing a shirt and tie for the occasion, awaiting the arrival of Princess Anne. I don't know how long they waited; Atkins and I gave it five minutes then left, a job well done.

****

July 2 2008. *PANACHE.*

If I have to make the short journey into the town centre and don't fancy walking I quite often use the local half-hourly bus service. Not only is it free to pensioners but it saves getting the car out and allows me to indulge in one of my favourite pastimes - listening in to people's conversations. Very often this is unrewarding, unless you're interested in the latest state of someone's haemorrhoids or the price of minced beef at Morrisons, but occasionally you hear a gem. I heard one this morning.

"Oh I like your hair," said the old dear.

"Do you like it?" said the other old dear seated next to her.

"Yes, it suits you. With your thin hair. Never been much body in your hair, has there."

"My mother was the same, my mother always had thin hair."

"I know. Where did you have it done?"

"That place on Union Road. Our Muriel put me on to it, they're ever so good and they give you a chocolate digestive with you tea."

"I like a nice chocolate digestive, I must give them a try. What are they called?

"Oh....What is it now?....my memory!....Hot Pot."

"Hot Pot? I've never seen a hairdresser's on called Hot Pot and I go down Union Road regular."

"No, not Hot Pot….. something like Hot Pot……..Tater pie.

"Tater pie?"

"No, hash. Tater hash."

"Tater hash?"

"No, but something very similar to …… Pan hash! That's it. Pan hash. Definitely."

"Pan hash?" The old dear thought for a moment, then said:" You mean *Panache* you silly old fool, it's pronounced *Panache*."

****

September 12 2008. *FAITH HEALER.*

I've suffered with anal pain for the last few years. It's bearable, but when it's bad it's as though someone is sticking the end of a cricket stump up my bottom. Thankfully it's only the blunt end as yet but that's bad enough. I've tried all sorts of things in the hope of getting rid of it; conventional medicine; acupuncture; homeopathy; hypnotherapy; aromatherapy: even therapy without a prefix; all to no avail. Last week I read in the local freebie newspaper that a faith healer, a travelling evangelist, was to visit the area. He would be attending the local Revivalist

124

Church next week and would be laying hands on and curing the illnesses and maladies of anyone who cared to come along. The bottom of the barrel having been reached, I went along, albeit more than a little-self consciously.

It is without a shadow of doubt the most weird, most embarrassing experience of my life, and we are talking here of a man who was once caught masturbating in the lavatory when he was fourteen years old by his nineteen-year-old sister.

The room in the Revivalist Church was almost full, at least a couple of hundred people seated on the twenty or so rows of forms that in the absence of pews provided the seating. Most of the people in attendance seemed to be fit and well, indeed hale and hearty, and almost all of them had a look about them, a joyful light in their eyes that seemed to say 'I've got religion'. I noted that the vast majority of them were women. I'm saying nothing.

In an effort to be as inconspicuous as possible I sat myself down on the back row. A man with even more joyful light in his eyes than the others immediately pounced on me and asked me if I'd come along to be cured. When I admitted I had he took me by the arm, dragged me to my feet and ushered me to the very front row. On the way there he told me he had seen the faith healer, Roy something or other he was called, Todd I think, perform his miracles on many occasions and he was sure he'd be able to help me no matter what was wrong with me. I might have shared his confidence if he hadn't walked with a pronounced limp. He sat me down next to another five people who had come along in the hope that the faith healer would be able to cure them of their afflictions.

The meeting commenced. The vicar, or whatever the Revivalists call their main man, the Head Reviver possibly, got things under way. No sooner had he welcomed everyone and gone into his sermon than a woman sprung to her feet and shouted "Hallelujah!" Then a man jumped up and shouted "Praise the Lord!" The Head Reviver smiled, looked fondly at we in the front row and explained. "That's how we do things here at the Revivalist Church. No one is afraid to express their feelings; if we feel the urge to praise the Lord we just do it, we don't hold back." This seemed to free-up a few more of the congregation, who were perhaps a bit more reticent than the ones who'd already let it all hang out, because almost immediately another four sprang to their feet and "Hallelujha'd" and "Praised the Lord."

This went on for the entire time the Head Reviver was speaking. At one point there were more people standing up and praising the Lord than there were sitting down and listening to the Head Reviver, who was by now wasting his time because even I couldn't hear him properly and I was only sat about a yard away. Then, to wild applause, the faith healer was introduced. When everyone had settled down he spoke of the last time he'd visited, some months previously, and of the people he'd cured on that occasion. Cue joyful shouts of "Hallelujah!" all round. He went on to regale the enthralled congregation with his recent exploits in America and beyond, as well as in this country, and told of the thousands of people he'd been able to help with the gift given to him by the good Lord, which all went down very well and brought forth even more 'Hallelujahs'.

He went on to ask if there was anyone here tonight who needed his help and if so would they stand up. Looking at each other a bit self-consciously, especially me and the severely bow-legged woman sat next to me - that'll test him I remember thinking - we got to our feet. The faith healer went to the first of us, the woman on my other side, asked her name and asked what was wrong with her. She said she had a chronic bad back. The faith healer laid a hand on her back and addressed the congregation. "Our comrade Jennifer has a chronic back condition. I want each and every one of you here tonight to concentrate as hard as you can on my hand so that the goodness given to you by the power of the Lord may course through it and into poor Jennifer's back." Total silence for about twenty seconds. I chanced a glance round. Every eye in the place was on the faith healer. Every face was wreathed in concentration, every brain summoning up the power of the Lord. The faith healer's eyes were cast heavenwards, his face a picture of both agony and ecstasy. He suddenly took a pace back, almost a stagger, as if knocked back, and shook his head as though trying to clear it. Then he looked at poor Jennifer, tenderly. "Tell me Jennifer, how is your back now?"

She put an explorative hand to it, moved it up and down a little. "It....it's a bit better," she said, a little unbelievingly, then, with more conviction. "It's a *lot* better. Yes, a lot better, I can hardly feel the pain at all now."

Gasps of incredulity from the congregation.

"That's the power of *the Lord'* the ecstatic faith healer proclaimed. "The power of the Lord has cured Jennifer's chronic bad back."

Wild applause, more "Hallelujahs and "Praise the Lords."

I was next in line. I must admit, having witnessed the miracle that had just taken place, that I had begun to have little more hope than previously. The faith healer turned to me and asked my name. I told him. "And what is wrong with you, Terry?" he asked. "I suffer from anal pain," I said. This seemed to throw him. Probably because it was the first time he'd ever been confronted with such an ailment.

"What?" he said.

"Anal pain," I repeated. I wasn't speaking very loudly as I was naturally feeling more than a little embarrassed about the whole thing, but quietly as I spoke the faith healer spoke even more quietly. "Is there anything else wrong with you?" he asked, in an almost furtive manner, tinged with hope.

"No" I said, "just the anal pain."

Even more embarrassed about it than I was, which is saying a lot, he turned to the congregation and said: "Terry has....a pain. I want each and every one of you to concentrate as hard as you can on my hand so that the goodness given to you by the power of the Lord will course through it and into Terry." Then he put his hand on my bottom. Gingerly is too positive an adjective for the manner in which he did this, and his hand wasn't there for anything near as long as it had been on poor Jennifer's back, about one nanosecond at the most I would guess. I was definitely short-changed on his trance-like state too - it was more a rolling of the eyes, in fact he may well have been rolling his eyes, I was certainly rolling mine - as he'd no sooner gone into it than he came out of it. Then he said, "I'm sure you'll be a lot better now" and moved on to the woman with the bow legs. When he saw her he almost came back to me but he was in luck because it turned out she'd come about her migraine.

I don't know if he managed to cure it because I'd had enough by then and headed for the exit. As I was going through the door a woman on the back row turned to another woman and said, "He's walking a lot better now isn't he."

November 30 2008. *SPORTSWRITER OF THE YEAR.*

Today, whilst in the dentist's waiting room waiting to have a tooth extracted, I came across an article in the Daily Telegraph in praise Michael Parkinson. Apparently he used to write a sports column for that newspaper and the article included extracts of his work. I read it through and a few minutes later had the tooth extracted and there is no doubt that the former experience was more enjoyable than the latter. This didn't surprise me at all, no more than the news that Parky was once 'Sportswriter of the Year'. Indeed if I were to be told he was the 'Sportswriter of the Century' I wouldn't question it, since if he is only half as good at sports writing as he was at fawning over film stars and pop personalities on his tiresome chat show then his sports-writing skills will be of the highest order: -

TV CLIP – PARKY IS WITH PAUL McCARTNEY.
PARKY: Sir Paul, it goes without saying that I have always been one of the greatest admirers of The Beatles since they emerged with such impact on the world of music in the early sixties, and although I'm not one to pick favourites if I were forced to pick my favourite Beatle I would in all honesty have to say it was you. So it gives me added pleasure that the song you have chosen to sing, nay honour us with tonight, is my very, very favourite Beatle number, your very own, quite wonderful, 'Yesterday'. But before you perform it, in your own inimitable style, could I trouble you Sir Paul, to drop your trousers, so that I can crawl up your arse physically as well as literally?"

But to return to Parky's 'Sportswriter of the Year' award. I mean what's that all about? An award just for doing your job? Why for God's sake? And it isn't just sportswriters who find it necessary to heap glory on themselves just for doing their jobs; the rest of the newspaper writing profession also find it irresistible; so we have a 'News Reporter of the Year' award, a 'Show Business Writer of the Year' award, a 'Fashion Writer of the Year' award, a 'Theatre Critic of the Year' award, etc, ad nauseum.

I can understand Film and TV stars showering themselves with awards such as Oscars and Baftas and Tonys and Emmys and whatever acronym they next come up with in order to honour themselves - probably the SAGAS, 'Shit Actor Great Acceptance Speech' - because by definition being an actor demands that you are a bit of a show-off. But journalists are supposed to be intelligent people and above such self-aggrandisement.

And if newspapers feel it necessary to garland their most accomplished practitioners with awards, why not other professions? Refuse collectors have collectively blotted their copybook since the advent of wheelie bins and the only award some of them deserve is the 'Order of the Boot', but if Sportswriter of the Year why not 'Ratcatcher of the Year', a far more deserving cause I would have thought. We can manage without newspaper columnists but a country without ratcatchers would soon find itself in more trouble than the Americans found themselves in in Vietnam. Hospital doctors are equally deserving of recognition. Fancy words in a newspaper are all well and good but of little use to you when you find yourself with a malignant tumour. Give me a man who knows how to deal with cancer of the colon than someone who knows how to use a semi-colon any day of the

130

week. Firemen are surely more worthy than journalists when it comes to the question of receiving recognition for their labours. There are many more examples; people serving in the armed forces, merchant seamen, bomb disposal experts, volunteer lifeboatmen, mountain rescue teams, the list is endless.

But hold on a minute; if these professions honoured their best who would report the matter? The newspapers? "What's that? A piece about the 'Ratcatcher of the Year'? Sorry, haven't the space, we're doing a two-page colour spread on the 'Award for the Newspaper Writer who Hasn't Won Any Other Newspaper Writing Awards'."

****

December 1 2008. *A BIZARRE INCIDENT.*

It was without any doubt the weirdest thing that anyone has ever said to me.
"I'm Harrop," the man said by way of introduction. "Harrop the Rapist.
I was travelling home on a train from Romiley, a small town a few miles away. The man got on at Marple, the next stop down the line. The carriage was almost empty, just two or three passengers. I'd chosen to sit at a seat with a table so I could rest my newspaper on it whilst doing the crossword. Despite their being plenty seating availably, including seats at an empty table, the man chose to sit opposite me. As he did I looked up from my crossword, we made eye contact, and he smiled and said it. "I'm Harrop. Harrop the Rapist."

I wasn't quick enough. Had I been I would have come back with, "I'm Ravenscroft. Ravenscroft the Man Who Goes about Cutting the Bollocks off Rapists with a Rusty Knife."

But his remark took me so much by surprise it rendered me temporarily speechless. I wondered what was the point of his saying it? To distinguish himself from, say, Harrop the Window Cleaner or Harrop the Travel Agent, maybe brothers of his, in much the same way that people in Wales are in the habit of calling themselves Jones the Butcher and Jones the Greengrocer, to set them apart from all the other Joneses.

He had said the words as though he spoke them often, and brightly, business-like, with no little pride in his voice, as though he might have done if he was telling me he was Harrop the Brain Surgeon or Harrop the Mountaineer, of Everest fame.

Thinking about it I suppose he said it because it must be his only claim to fame. The poor bastard. I almost felt sorry for him. Only almost, though.

I was considering giving him a hefty kick under the table, then apologising, saying I couldn't help it, it was an ailment I had, named after me in fact, 'Ravenscroft's Kicking Twats under the Table Syndrome', when he got up and got off at the next stop.

****

December 3 2008. *PIG SICK.*

Atkins is a dab hand at shooting rabbits, his skill with the twelve bore shotgun having provided dinner for The Trouble and me on numerous occasions. Consequently he spends a good deal of his leisure hours in the heather and gorse-strewn countryside that surrounds our little town in making the local population of rabbits a little less abundant.

Unfortunately some of the surrounding countryside, in addition to the heather and gorse and rabbits, also contains farms, and it was at one of these farms a couple of days ago that Atkins, in addition to bagging a rabbit, also bagged a large pig that happened to be careless enough to be standing directly behind the rabbit when he let rip with his shotgun. It was a complete accident of course, but conscious of the fact that the farmer might not take too kindly to the premature slaying of one of his porkers Atkins hopped it from the scene of the crime without further ado, but with great haste.

That might have been the end of the matter but apparently someone observed the dastardly deed and reported it to the farmer. Subsequently the farmer, seeking compensation for his loss, took Atkins to task about it. Naturally Atkins denied all knowledge of the matter, telling the farmer that at the time of the alleged incident he was with me, some ten miles away, on a fishing trip. He knew that the farmer would waste no time in calling on me to confirm his alibi, so once the farmer had departed Atkins called me, told me about the escapade, and asked me to support his story. I agreed of course; Atkins was a friend in need.

I am not a great fan of farmers. I don't much care for the way they are always pleading poverty whilst availing themselves of the very latest in 4 X 4 off road gas guzzling ego- massaging wank tanks. As Atkins succinctly once put it himself, "You don't see many farmers riding around on a bike." So there was never any question that I wouldn't back up my friend's deceit, and in doing so get him off the hook. Until the time the farmer came knocking on my door this morning I had scarcely stopped thinking about poor old

Atkins shooting the pig. I just couldn't get it out of my head and had several times burst out laughing at the image it conjured up. When I tried to read my book the words just disappeared to be replaced by a picture of Atkins and the pig. I even tried watching a play on TV, Martin Clunes in some nonsense or other, but even then I kept getting this vision of a pig on the screen every few minutes, a situation not helped by Martin Clunes, an actor who has taken on an increasingly porcine-like appearance the older and more famous he has become.

This morning at breakfast I was still chuckling about it. The Trouble asked me what it was I found so funny and when I told her she couldn't stop chuckling about it either, and set me off chuckling again. Consequently when the farmer called, in a 58 plate Range Rover of course, I could barely keep my face straight. The farmer's face was very straight, but then he'd just lost a pig. He came straight to the point. "Do you know a Richard Atkins?"

"Ah," I replied immediately, "You mean Atkins the pig shooter."

Why I said it I will never know. I certainly didn't want to get Atkins in any more trouble than he was in already. The only thing I can put it down to is that over the last couple of days I'd thought so much about Atkins shooting the pig that when his name was mentioned I immediately associated it with his pig shooting exploits. And that, coupled with the incident the other day with Harrop the Rapist, had perhaps led me to automatically attach a wrong-doers crime to his name.

Anyway the upshot of it was that I had to tell Atkins I'd accidentally shopped him. He was quite livid, as could be well understood. However after I offered to go halves with him on the compensation demanded by the farmer he came round a bit, but our friendship may be a little fragile for a while. And we claimed the pig of course. We'll be eating pork for weeks.

****

December 16 2008. *POLES.*

Just recently our town has seen an influx of Poles. Not poles as in telegraph poles or flag poles or even the poles that nubile young ladies use in the performance of erotic dancing for the amusement of randy businessmen, but Poles as in natives of a large, cold, East European country. The attraction for British factory owners is of course cheap labour, and for the Poles the chance to earn a decent living without the risk of having their extremities frozen solid whilst doing it.

We've welcomed about a hundred of them thus far and all have soon found jobs, a good proportion of them at the local sweet factory, Swizzels/Matlow. Swizzels are of course the manufacturers of the famous 'Love Hearts', the sweets that have mottos such as 'I Love You' and 'Be My Angel'. Or at least they did when they were first introduced. Nowadays along with the original messages they also bear more risqué mottos such as 'Hello Big Boy' and 'Lovely Bum'. With the addition of Poles to the workforce I don't suppose it will be long before we see the introduction of a 'Lick My Pole' Love Heart. But at least the Poles won't be opening up restaurants like the Indians and Chinese and Italians, not unless the British public suddenly develop a taste for beetroot, cabbage soup and lard sandwiches that is.

I came across my first Pole yesterday, although I didn't realise he was a Pole at first. He was half of the two-man

135

team at a recently opened hand car wash. I found out after he and his mate had washed my car and his mate had gone off for change from the ten pound note I'd offered in payment.

"Weather's bucking up a bit at last," I said, passing the time of day as you do. He just smiled at me. I thought maybe he was a bit shy. I tried again. "Not doing too well at the cricket, are we." Nothing. Not even a smile this time. Not a cricket fan then. I tried a third time. "Who's going to win the Cup this year then?"

"No spik Englis," he said. "Pole."

What could I say? The only word I know in Polish is 'Polish' and I'm not at all sure 'Polish' is Polish in Poland, it could be Polszkygnkzch or some other such name with very few vowels and loads of k's and z's. I thought about and finally pointed to myself and said: "No spik Polish. Englis."

He smiled and offered his hand. I shook it. Contact had been made. For some strange reason it made me happy. I must be getting soft in my old age.

****

December 20 2008. *THE SONIC YARD PROTECTOR.*

The advert in the small ads section of the newspaper read - '24 Hour Protection against Unwanted Animal Intruders. Simply place the Sonic Yard Protector in your garden and repel foxes, dogs, cats, rabbits, squirrels, rodents, insects and more! The new Sonic Yard Protector broadcasts a powerful, continuous ultrasonic pulse that will irritate animal pests and drive them away. It also has a built-in PIR motion detector which will sense any animal intruder's movement and activate the system to emit an owl sound'.

I read it twice. There was something wrong with the advert but I couldn't put my finger on it. Not to worry, I thought, the Sonic Yard Protector is just the sort of thing I need to keep the neighbourhood's cats out of my back garden, which they have recently taken to using as a meeting place, and promptly sent off for one.

I should have worried; although, true to its promise, the Sonic Yard Protector kept away everything it claimed to keep away. In fact since I erected it we have had in our garden not a single, cat, dog, rabbit, squirrel or fox, leastwise not during the hours of daylight. What we have had however, and still have, is an owl. A particularly loud owl. And when we got the owl I realised what it was that was wrong with the advert; for if, as it claimed, the Sonic Yard Protector kept out all uninvited cats, dogs, etc, why then would you need its built-in PIR motion detector to sense any intruding animal movements and activate the system to emit an owl sound? Because if the Sonic Yard Protector was doing its job there wouldn't *be* any intruding animals to protect against.

The Trouble and I were first woken by the hooting of the owl at one-o-clock in the morning. Well at least we knew the owl sound worked, we consoled ourselves. We knew it again when it woke us up again an hour later. The following night it woke us up at 12.30 a.m. then again at half past three. The second time it woke us up there wasn't one owl hooting but two. I looked out of the bedroom window. There, as large as life, was an owl perched on the garden shed, |next to the Sonic Yard Protector. The bloody thing had attracted it! The following day I took the Sonic Yard Protector down before the owl found a way of mating with it and we ended up with a garden full of owls. But now the owl keeps coming back.

Looking for its mate I suppose. So now we are awoken in the middle of the night by a real owl. And during the day we have a garden full of cats again.

I believe that owls are a protected species. All I can say is I hope the protection comes in the form of a bulletproof vest because if it keeps coming for much longer I'm going to get Atkins to shoot it.

****

December 22 2008. *POLE-AXED.*

Thanks to my meeting the friendly Pole in the car wash a few days ago Atkins and I have a new daft game. It's called 'Pretending to be Polish' and we played it for the first time today during the half- hour train journey to Manchester.

During the off-peak hours the trains are emptier than a politician's promise so as usual we had the whole coach to ourselves.

The game started when the conductor came round shortly after we'd boarded the train. "Tickets please," he announced cheerily. He didn't stay cheery for long.

"Warsaw," I said, taking out my wallet.

"Pardon?"

"Warsaw. Come back Englands."

"Return," Atkins explained. "He mean Warsaw return."

"We don't go to Warsaw. Manchester, that's where we go."

"Warsaw," I repeated, a little more firmly, taking a fiver from my wallet and waving it. "Come back Englands"

"We don't go to Warsaw," said the Conductor, speaking slowly for my benefit. "We only go to Piccadilly."

"Piccalilli? Nice on Spam.

138

"Piccadilly! It's the terminus!"

"Terminus?"

Atkins came to the rescue again. He pointed to me. "Pole." Then he pointed to himself. "Pole." Then he held up two fingers. "Three Poles. No spik English gut. No understand."

"Warsaw," I said, pushing the fiver into the conductor's hand. "Come backs."

"For the last time we don't go to fucking Warsaw," said the no longer cheery Conductor.

Atkins's face lit up. "Understand Fucking," he said. "Fucking awful weather. Fucking Monday morning again. Fucking scouse bastards!"

"Warsaw," I said. "No Piccalilli."

The Conductor took great pains to spell it out slowly. We..do..not..go..Warsaw! Go..Manchester!"

The Conductor's slowly enunciated words obviously made sense to my fellow Pole because Atkins now gave a huge beam. "Go Manchester!" he said. The Conductor smiled. Atkins continued. "Go Manchester United! Man United go! Go Wayne Rooney, Go Ryan Giggs, Please don't take our Socks Jar away."

"Red Navy!" I said.

"Army," said Atkins.

"Army Navy!" I said.

"Army Navy Store," said Atkins.

"Oh fuck this for a game of soldiers ," said the conductor, and went on his way.

We got away with the fare too.

****

139

April 10 2009. *BABY ON BOARD.*

Today I saw another of those 'Baby On Board' stickers that clutter up the back windows of cars. What purpose do they serve? Does the owner of the car maybe expect you to stop them and ask for a look at their darling little pride and joy?

"Why have you stopped me?"

"I'd like a look at your baby."

"A look at my baby?"

"Well why else would you be advertising that you're carrying your baby in your car if it isn't so people can stop you to have a look at it?"

Maybe it isn't that. Maybe the stickers are designed to influence the decision of the driver in the car behind as to whether or not they should crash into the car in front of him.

"Oh look Ethel, I see there's a 'Baby on Board' sticker on the car in front, I was about to recklessly plough into the back of it but now I've been warned there's a baby on board I'm going to take avoiding action."

I don't think so. For surely anyone about to plough into the back of a car would already have taken all the avoiding action they can, whether the car in front is sporting a 'Baby on Board' sticker on the rear window or not.

When I first saw one of the stickers I thought it had perhaps been put there to warn the driver of the car behind not to get too close as in addition to any other people who might be on board there was also a baby, therefore one should be especially careful. But I soon dismissed that theory, common sense telling me that if you're near enough to a car to read the sticker you're already much nearer to it than safe braking distance will allow, even at only thirty miles-an-hour.

In fact, women being the way they are about babies, you might think a 'Baby on Board' sticker would be more likely to cause an accident than prevent one - for what woman does not like to look at a baby? And if that's the case what then are the chances of a woman driver, on observing that the car in front is displaying a 'Baby on Board' sticker, and in her eagerness to see the baby, getting too close to it and crashing into the back of it? I don't think BetFred would give you very generous odds against it happening.

"You're driving too close to that car in front, Ethel."

"But I want to see the baby."

CRASH!

"I think that's it there, Ethel, the one with the busted head and the rattle."

On thinking about it I've reached the conclusion that it must be some sort of announcement - the mother, now swollen with pride instead of the baby, proclaiming to the world that she has now had the baby, but at this moment isn't out with it showing it off to her friends, or pushing it around in its trendy three-wheeler pram, or has it slung to her front like some tiny mountaineer trying to scale the twin peaks of Mount Tits, but has her new pride and joy in the car with her, where it can't for the moment be admired by everyone. So she has to tell everyone. "Baby on Board!"

I noticed recently that there are now adaptations of this ubiquitous sticker. One such is: 'Small Person on Board'. The first time I saw one I thought at first it meant the car was being driven by a midget and was a variation on the Long Vehicle/Short Vehicle sticker joke, but on looking inside the car saw that the small person referred to was a toddler. Since then I've seen quite a few 'Small Person on Board' stickers. And two or three 'Cheeky Little Monkey on Board' stickers.

I have not however, as might be expected, all children by no means being little angels, see any 'Little Horror on Board' or 'Whingeing Little Twat on Board' stickers. There is obviously a gap in the market here. I don't suppose it will be long before someone fills it.

****

April 25 2009. *THE WOMAN FROM GLOSSOP.*

On a flight home from Lanzarote, due to a mix-up at the check-in desk, The Trouble and I were split up and I found myself seated next to a Woman from Glossop who spent the entire flight telling the man seated the other side of her all about her timeshare apartment in Puerto del Carmen, the main resort in Lanzarote.

Like me the Woman from Glossop had been split up from her spouse on the flight but apparently this had been arranged by design rather than by accident as "We always sit apart on flights as we see enough of each other while we're in Lanzarote." I have little doubt it was the Man from Glossop who insisted on these travelling arrangements, indeed if I had been he not only would I have insisted on a separate seat but it would have been on a separate aeroplane. Prior to the flight I knew next to nothing about timeshare apartments, which is about as much as I want to know, but by the time we'd landed at Manchester Airport about a million hours later the Woman from Glossop had ensured that I knew much more about them than I wanted to know, to the power of ten.

Her current apartment, 'south-facing, veranda, two bedrooms both with en-suite, loads of storage space and a communion pool - I think she meant communal pool, but

142

you never know, perhaps the timeshare complex has a resident vicar and they have a 'Baptism 'n Barbecue Night' - was her third, all of them in Puerto del Carmen, the present one acquired in 1999, the first - no en-suite unfortunately, but a bidet - acquired in 1985. At first the Woman from Glossop had just the one week's timeshare entitlement per year but by now she and the Man from Glossop were up to six weeks per year, in two week segments. During the last twenty-three years they had never been anywhere else for a holiday other than to their timeshare apartment in Lanzarote.

Now I've got nothing against Lanzarote - you're certainly not going to die from over-excitement there but in a clean, easy going, always nice weather, not-too-many-Germans sort of place, it is ideal. But six weeks there every year? While places such as Provence and Tuscany and the Greek Islands remain as unvisited as a virgin's vagina?

I learned that for the remaining forty-six weeks of the year the Woman from Glossop and the Man from Glossop spend their time in Glossop, saving up like mad to spend the other six weeks in Lanzarote. They never go anywhere else, so the Woman from Glossop informed the Man not from Glossop seated the other side of her, because if they did they wouldn't be able to afford their full quota of six weeks in Lanzarote. Now I've been to Glossop, and while it is by no means the worst place I have ever been to – I once went to Rotherham - it is certainly not the sort of place you would wish to spend forty-six weeks of the year in.

Yet this couple have deliberately chosen to live out their lives in it for forty-six weeks in every year, and the other six weeks in Lanzarote. Nowhere else on Earth existed for them. Their entire life consisted of being in Glossop, or in Lanzarote, or on the twenty-five mile stretch of road between

Glossop and Manchester Airport, a road only slightly more enjoyment-fulfilling than the road to perdition.

Is it possible that anyone could credit this? They had deliberately consigned themselves to a world without France and Italy and Greece, a world where the Lake District and the Cotswolds and the Yorkshire Dales don't exist, a place where Edinburgh Castle and York Minster and Stonehenge might just as well be on the Moon. What sort of person can do this? The mind boggles. Mine did, on the flight back. And whilst it was boggling I fell asleep and thankfully didn't wake up until we had started the descent to Manchester Airport. When I did The Woman from Glossop was telling the Man not from Glossop that next year she and the Man from Glossop hoped to be going to Lanzarote for *seven* weeks. Still, looking on the bright side, that's one less week in Glossop.

****

May 27 2009. *THE NATION'S FAVOURITE.*

Once again I have been lumped together with all the rest of the people in Britain and informed that someone is my favourite something or other. You know the sort of thing, you read it in the newspapers all the time – 'Trevor McDonald, the nation's favourite newscaster', 'Cilla Black, the nation's favourite auntie', 'Sean Connery, the nation's favourite Scotsman'; not forgetting the one we used to get once a week on average until she popped her clogs, 'The Queen Mother, the nation's favourite granny'.

I once read that Michael Barrymore was 'the nation's favourite funnyman'. I doubt very much if he was the

144

favourite of the poor sod who died in his swimming pool and while he was drowning he thought it was funny.

This time it is Cliff Richard, who I am informed is 'the Nation's favourite Oldie'. Well I am a member of our nation and he certainly isn't *my* favourite oldie. I know a lot of Oldies who I prefer to Cliff Richard. In fact I know a lot of Richards who I prefer to Cliff Richard - Keith Richards, Viv Richards, Little Richard and Richard Branson, being just four of them. Nor is Trevor McDonald my favourite newscaster (John Suchet), my favourite auntie Cilla Black (my Auntie Annie) nor Sean Connery my favourite Scotsman (Billy Connolly). And the Queen Mother was certainly not my favourite granny. In fact had there been ten million grannies resident in Britain when the Queen Mother's extravagances were still a drain on the taxpayer then she would have been my ten millionth favourite granny, and only then because there weren't ten million and one grannies, even if the additional granny had been Granny 'Chainsaw Anna' Hargreaves.

****

June 2 2009. *POTTERING ABOUT.*

I can't recall in which book I first came across the expression 'pottering about in the garden', but it was probably in one of the Just William books or maybe The Famous Five series I read when I first became interested in reading when I was aged about twelve. I was attracted to the phrase at once; it sounded such a cosy, English, way in which to occupy oneself, and I couldn't wait until I was a grown up and would be able to potter about in a garden myself (I assumed that children couldn't potter about in the garden because whenever I came across the phrase it was always being done by an adult, invariably an old one).

In those days I couldn't even pretend, as children do, to potter about in the garden; we lived in a mean terraced house which didn't have a garden in which to potter, just paving stones at the front of the house and a backyard hardly big enough to swing a landlord in. So when I married The Trouble and we eventually got a house of our own, with a small garden, I was naturally eager to get some pottering time in.

It never happened. Since I first ventured into a garden all those years ago with a virgin spade and un-calloused hands I have never once pottered. I have potted. And I have dug, double-dug, forked, raked, hoed, chopped, sawed and hammered, all of which are far too strenuous activities to be called pottering, which is defined in the dictionary as 'to busy oneself in a mild way with trifling tasks'. I have mown lawns, trimmed hedges, turned over flower beds, laid paving stones, humped bags of compost and fertilizers, and in the course of this have been bitten by ants and stung by wasps, bees and hornets, and on one occasion savaged by a stray dog; none of which can remotely be termed as mild or trifling.

It eventually dawned on me that there was no such thing as pottering about in the garden, except in books, and that I never would potter, that I would go through life as a non-potterer. Until yesterday.

I'd been giving the garden a general tidying up, uprooting triffids and other monster-like weeds that had sprung up in the borders, like they do, preparatory to planting something more colourful and less invasive. One of the weeds was particularly hard to dislodge. I took a firm hold of it, braced myself, gave an almighty heave….and it shot out of the ground much more easily than I had bargained for and sent me staggering back a couple of steps. The second of the steps caused me to put my foot onto the business end of a garden rake I'd carelessly left on the ground and the other end of it shot up and cracked me a nasty blow on the side of the head, gashing my temple. When I'd stopped hollering and seeing stars I went into the kitchen to attend to it. The Trouble was one the phone. "Your dad?" she said, to whoever was on the other end of the phone, either my son or one of my daughters, "Oh, he's pottering about in the garden."

****

June 10 2009. *SNOOKERED.*

About twenty years ago, when I was scriptwriting and travelling down to London on a regular basis, the train stopped to pick up at Stoke-on-Trent as usual. However, far from usual, who should board the train and sit down opposite me but snooker star Ray Reardon, who was then the current world champion. With him he had a long, thin tube, which obviously contained his snooker cue - unless he had a very thin wife he wanted to keep hidden from sight - so he was probably on his way to take part in a competition, or maybe play an exhibition match. As he took his seat I made eye contact with him and gave him a friendly smile, which he returned. I leaned forward slightly to look at him more closely and allowed the light of recognition to illuminate my face. "Excuse me," I said, and then as I paused for effect I saw in his face just the faintest look of 'Oh here we go again,

147

another fan who's going to be asking me all the ins-and-outs of what it's like to be a famous snooker player'. However I wasn't going to let that stop me. "I hope you don't mind my mentioning it," I went on, "But....aren't you Hurricane Higgins?"

He saw the joke and laughed generously. We chatted for a while. Ray of course, due to his dark-eyed sallow features and jet black hair with its prominent widow's peak was known throughout the snooker world by the nickname 'Dracula', but I must say I found him to be a perfect gentleman and he didn't bite me once. He laughed again when I mentioned that I enjoyed a game of snooker myself and told of the day I'd been playing in my local club and had compiled a break of thirty-six when I suddenly broke off and walked over to a yucca tree standing in the corner, which I then proceeded to stare at with great concentration. "Why did you do that?" he asked.

"I was looking at a plant." I said.

That joke started life as what is known in the comedy scriptwriting world as a 'quickie', a very short sketch, usually just a set-up followed by a punch line or dramatic twist. Sometime previously I'd sent it in to one or other of the many sketch shows that were on television in those days. It was used but I can't remember by which show. One 'snooker' quickie I sent in which wasn't used, probably on the grounds of cost, was when the previously mentioned Alex 'Hurricane' Higgins won the World Championship at the Crucible in Sheffield and immediately after being presented with the trophy was joined on camera by his pretty young wife, carrying their new-born baby. My idea was to re-enact this scene but have the winner of the trophy joined by about twenty more pretty young women carrying babies in their arms.

I was reminded of the Ray Reardon incident when I was channel-hopping tonight, trying to find something on the TV that I could bear to watch - usually a forlorn hope - when I lighted on the snooker. There was a time when I could pass a pleasant hour with televised snooker, in the days when it was only on for an hour, but that isn't the case nowadays, it's on for hour after hour after interminable hour, television as usual, having given birth to a good idea, then proceeding to strangle the life out of it through over-exposure. I might just possibly have watched it for a bit had anyone actually been playing snooker but these days they spend more time talking about it than playing it, which is what they were doing when I zapped on to it.

"Oh for Christ's sake shut up!" I said to John Virgo.

"He can't hear you, you know," said The Trouble.

"It wouldn't make any difference if he could, he'd still keep on talking" I replied, zapping John Virgo into oblivion, which is just about the best place for him and the Scottish woman who does chirpy he was 'chatting' to.

"I don't understand you," said The Trouble. "If you don't like what's on the television why don't you just do something else instead of talking to it?"

"I like talking to it."

The Television now joined in our conversation. "And now it's time for EastEnders," it said.

"Oh no it bloody isn't," I said. ZAP!

The Trouble looked up from her magazine. "Why don't you just switch it off? Instead of switching from channel to channel all the time? That remote doesn't know whether it's coming or going."

"It's going. On the tip with the telly if they don't start putting some decent programmes on."

"You said that last week but you keep watching it."

"Only in the way that Captain Bligh kept scanning the horizon when he was cast adrift on an open boat; in the hope that if I keep looking I might one day finally see land."

"There's plenty of land to be seen now if you'd look properly."

The Shakespeare in me emerged, probably because I'd just zapped off yet another showing of 'Shakespeare in Love'. "What land is this of which you speak?"

"Well there's 'The Royal'."

At first I thought she meant a documentary about the Queen or one of her flawed offspring, then I realised she meant the hospital thing on Sunday nights, a soap-ish drama whose only redeeming feature is the sixties music that punctuates the scenes. "The Royal?" I said. "The Royal isn't land. Or if it is it's a swamp. I wish it was a swamp then Wendy Craig might fall into it and be sucked under, I saw quite enough of her in fucking Butterflies."

"Fucking Butterflies? Wasn't that one of David Attenborough's?"

"Bill Oddie I think."

"He's never off the box these days, is he."

"He should be in a box. With Wendy Craig."

"Oh I quite like him."

"He's a self-satisfied pretentious little prick. Like Noel Edmonds."

"Don't you like anybody on television?"

I thought about it for a moment. "I quite like one of the presenters." I don't, I was lying, I don't like any of them, especially Trevor McDonald, the lot of them would be knackered without the autocue, but I wanted to keep the conversation going. Television hasn't killed the art of conversation in our house. It fuels it.

****

June 18 2009. *FREE CDs.*

After a late breakfast I strolled along to the public library, conveniently only a couple of minutes away, to read the morning newspapers. I can afford to buy my own paper but I stopped buying one a year ago on principle.

About eighteen months prior to that I received a free music CD, 'Tom Jones and Friends', along with my morning paper. It was quite a surprise because I wasn't aware that Tom Jones had any friends, the Welshman being the owner of a voice designed to make enemies rather than cultivate friendships, but there you go. I looked at the cover. The first song was Tom Jones singing 'It's Not Unusual'. The second song was Engelbert Humperdinck singing 'Please Release Me'. Next up was Tom Jones singing 'The Green Green Grass of Home'. Next was Wilson Pickett with 'In the Midnight Hour'. Next was Tom Jones singing....well you get the idea.

There were twelve tracks on the CD, six by Tom Jones and six by six other artists. Now I might be a bit naïve but I would have expected an album called Tom Jones and Friends to consist of songs sung by Tom Jones accompanied by his friends, but apparently not. Tom Jones and Friends indeed! Who do they think they're kidding? I wouldn't mind betting that Tom Jones has never even met half the people on the CD and in all probability has never even heard of the singer of the final track, Hoagy Carmichael singing 'Stardust'.

Actually I would have quite liked to listen to Wilson Picket singing 'In the Midnight Hour' but not at the expense of having to listen to Tom Jones so I threw it in the bin.

I wouldn't have thought it possible that there was a less sick bucket-inducing CD than 'Tom Jones and Friends' but a couple of months later one turned up secreted in the pages of my newspaper. 'Engelbert Humperdinck and Friends'. The first track was Engelbert Humperdinck singing 'Please Release Me', the second track was Tom Jones singing 'It's Not Unusual', the third was Engelbert Humperdinck singing 'The Last Waltz'....surprise, surprise, there were six songs by Engelbert Humperdinck and six by six other artists. I threw it in the bin. My privilege. Besides, like the Tom Jones and Friends CD, it hadn't cost me anything, it was no skin off my nose. Two weeks later my newspaper went up by 3 p. Due to rising production costs.

A few weeks went by and I received another free CD, 'Twenty Golden Disco. It went straight in the bin. Over the next twelve months I received another three CDs. All unwanted. All unplayed. All binned. Two weeks later my newspaper went up another 2p due to rising production costs. The penny dropped. Could these rising production costs have anything to do with the costs of producing CDs of Tom Jones and Friends and all the other unasked for and unwanted CDs that had been forced on me over the last few months? Does the Pope shit in the woods? Far from it not being any skin off my nose it was by now a wonder I had any skin left on it . I cancelled my newspaper.

I had thrown every one of the CDs I received in the bin, as I suspect most people do. People who like Tom Jones already have CDs of him warbling his songs (they also have my sympathy), likewise Engelbert Humperdinck, likewise all the other artists on the 'free' CDs all the newspapers give away nowadays, so they are of no benefit to anyone whatsoever. Except of course the artists on the CDs, in the form of royalties, and the newspapers, in extra revenue every time they put up the price of their newspaper. But that doesn't bother me anymore because I've stopped buying them, apart from the Sunday Times, and I wouldn't buy that if it's countless unread supplements didn't provide excellent bulk for my compost bin

****.

July 3 2009. *IDIOT-PROOF.*

Atkins and I have another new daft game, albeit one with limited opportunities for playing it often, if ever again. In it Atkins takes the part of someone who isn't quite all there - not much acting ability needed there then - whilst I take the part of his carer. I dreamed it up this morning after I'd I passed a shop that sold cameras and telescopes; a large 'Sale' sign in the window had attracted my attention and I'd stopped to see what they had as I'm on the lookout for a pair of zoom lens binoculars. There weren't any but there was something far better. A bit of fun. In the form of a small camera, on offer at £10.99, which was claimed, according to its sale sticker, to be idiot-proof.

Before anyone else could snaffle it up I immediately called in on Atkins, and twenty minutes later we were in the shop asking to see the idiot-proof camera. The assistant got the camera out of the window and placed it on the counter for our consideration. "There you go."

I put on a doubtful expression. "It is idiot-proof, is it?"

"Oh absolutely."

Atkins looked at the camera in wide-eyed wonderment then turned to the assistant and said, like a little boy in a pet shop asking if he could hold a puppy, "Could I pick it up please?"

"Jimmy is on day release from the psychiatric wing of the hospital," I explained, in suitably sympathetic tones.

"Ah." The assistant nodded knowingly. He didn't know anything, poor bugger. "Of course you can pick it up, Jimmy," he said to Atkins, treating him to an avuncular smile.

Atkins picked up the camera, examined it briefly in wide-eyed wonder, then smashed it down as hard as he could on the counter top. The first time he did it probably rendered the camera beyond repair, and didn't do the counter much good either, but just in case it hadn't he repeated the treatment two more times in quick succession, and dropped it on the counter. It sat there looking like something that had just lost an argument with a sledgehammer.

Atkins looked at me in surprise. "It broke, Arthur," he said. "Camera broke."

My brow furrowed in a frown. "Yes, Jimmy." I turned to the assistant. "I thought you told me it was idiot-proof?"

The man was in a state of shock. He just stood with his mouth open, looking at Atkins and pointing at him.

"I said I thought you said the camera was idiot-proof," I persisted, this time allowing a little testiness to creep into my tone of voice.

154

"But....but he smashed it," the assistant said, still quite unable to believe what he had witnessed. "He smashed it to bits."

"Well of course he did," I said. "He's an idiot. That's what idiots do."

"I'm an idiot," grinned Atkins. He picked up a piece of the camera and examined it. "Camera no good now Arthur," he pronounced, wisely.

"Not much good in the first place if you ask me, Jimmy," I said, with a meaningful look at the assistant. "And certainly not idiot-proof, as claimed." I took Atkins by the arm. "Come along, we'll try Boots, I believe they do a good throw-away camera."

"Can Jimmy throw it away?" said Atkins. "Jimmy likes throwing things."

We left the shop without looking back. Five yards down the road I thought I heard a shout of "Hey, come back here!" from the shop but I probably imagined it.

****

August 22 2009. *VACU VIN.*

I don't know how many sad people there are in the world but it is over twenty five million. I don't mean sad 'miserable' I mean sad 'pathetic'. How do I know this? Read on.

Having picked up a magazine in the doctor's waiting room yesterday and reading that Mafeking had been relieved I looked around for a periodical that might be a bit more up-to-date. Finding one and glancing through it I saw an advertisement for a Vacu Vin. If you have never heard of a Vacu Vin, and I sincerely hope you haven't and never will, it is apparently a device that you insert into the neck of an

155

opened wine bottle in order to prevent the wine from oxidising if, in the words of the manufacturer of the Vacu Vin, 'you don't want to finish the bottle'.

If you don't want to finish the bottle? Bacchus would turn in his grave. I can honestly say that I have never once in my sixty-eight years on this Earth, forty-odd of them as a regular wine drinker, opened a decent bottle of wine and not wanted to finish it. Furthermore I can't visualise the time when I ever will open a decent bottle of wine and not want to finish it. Indeed if you were to try to stop me finishing it once I had opened it you would have to fight me, and you'd better be good because if in danger of losing my bottle of instant happiness I would fight you tooth and nail. Only the intervention of death would stop me finishing a decent bottle of wine once I'd opened it, and even then it would have to be a quick death or I would breathe my last along with the dregs from the bottom of the bottle.

Conversely I have quite often opened a crap bottle of wine and not wanted to finish it. Sometimes because it was oxidised, but more likely because it was some Australian rubbish I had been conned into buying through reading an over-enthusiastic review from some wine writer who should know better. However in those cases whilst it is true to say I didn't want to finish it, it is equally true that I didn't want to keep it either, I wanted to pour it down the sink, so why then would I need a Vacu Vin?

Surely nobody had been daft enough to buy such a totally useless article? When I got home I got Vacu Vin's number from what passes as Directory Enquiries nowadays and gave them a ring. I asked them if they'd ever sold any. They had. Up to press they "had sold over twenty five million of them, worldwide, since they were first introduced."

And that's why I know there are over twenty five million sad people in the world; because what else would a person be if not sad if they didn't want to finish a bottle of wine once they'd opened it?

Writing this has made me sad (sad 'miserable', not sad 'pathetic'), so I am now going to open a bottle of wine and drown my sorrows in it. And I will definitely not be needing a Vacu Vin as it's a nice burgundy I've tried before.

****

October 21 2009. *THE PLUMBER.*

I handed the plumber the cheque. He had repaired my leaking hot water cistern three weeks after the date he'd promised and his bill was only two and a half times more than I thought it would be, so all things considered I'd got off lightly. He put the cheque in his wallet, pushing aside a wad of notes thick enough to choke a donkey to make room for it, then went on his way as happy as a sandboy, or maybe that should be as happy as a plumber since plumbers are probably a lot happier than sandboys nowadays, leastwise they should be the prices they charge.

If I were asked to offer just one piece of advice to schoolchildren on which career to take up on leaving school I would tell them to rid their minds of all thoughts of entering the world of Information Technology and other computer-based vocations, and become a plumber. The advice, should things carry on the way they have been doing for the past fifteen or so years, would be ignored. I don't have access to the official figures but I would be very surprised if they weren't something like 'School-leavers wishing to sit at a computer with a mouse, thousands upon thousands', 'School-leavers wishing to sit at a cistern with a monkey wrench, nil'.

Why is this? Plumbers have got everything, but everything, going for them. The customer is entirely at his mercy. He can come and go whenever he pleases, and does. He can tell you that he's definitely coming on Monday and turn up indefinitely on Friday, and does. And if and when he does come he can charge you as much as he likes, and does. He can make a fortune, and does. Mine turned up in a brand new BMW with a 'My other car is a Rolls-Royce' sticker in the back window and I'm not at all sure he was joking.

And becoming a plumber is comparatively easy. It takes no great talent. It isn't, as they say, rocket science. Just a very basic knowledge of mathematics, a reasonably fit body, a little mechanical aptitude and the ability to drink gallons of tea. Even a plumber with only the most basic plumbing skills can make a very handsome living indeed, especially if he's mastered the only thing absolutely necessary if one is to become a success at his trade - the sharp intake of breath. This is the device which allows him, without question, to multiply the cost of whatever he is doing by a factor of between 2 and 10, depending upon the degree of sharpness exhibited in the intake of breath, and how much shaking of the head and tut-tutting accompanies it. We've all been there:-

You: "So how much is it going to set me back then?"

Plumber: (A SUDDEN SHARP INTAKE OF BREATH ACCOMPANIED BY MUCH SHAKING OF THE HEAD AND TUT-TUTTING) "Well it's a much bigger job than it looks, Squire."

Goodbye to that weekend in the Lake District you thought you could afford and hello to rip-off time.

About a minute after the plumber had left he was back at the front door. He had his bill in his hand. I thought I'd paid him an arm and a leg but I was wrong, I'd only paid him an arm. The leg was to come. It came. "I forgot to put the VAT on," he said. "Sorry." Not as sorry as me he wasn't.

****

December 12 2009. *CHRISTMAS CAROLS.*

It's Christmas time once again, and of course with the season of goodwill to all men comes Christmas Carols.

Once upon a time when the world was a more innocent place and people were less devious carol singers would start to sing their carol outside your door, then after a few lines (of the carol, not cocaine, these were innocent times remember) one of them would ring your bell. You then had a choice - to answer the door, listen to their merry carolling, then give them a Christmas box and perhaps invite them in for mince pies and sherry. Or, much more likely, pretend you weren't in, thus saving yourself a few bob.

Nowadays this isn't possible. Nowadays carollers, wise to the fact that you will probably try to pretend you aren't in, ring your doorbell and wait until you answer the door before they start singing, thus putting you in the position of having to give them a Christmas box or trundle out some excuse about not having any change and subsequently having your front door kicked in or your doorstep shat on or your garden gnome beheaded and thrown into your goldfish pond or some other act of wilful reprisal.

I have put in some thought over the past twelve months as to how I might overcome this problem, and at the eleventh hour - well it was around three-o-clock yesterday afternoon actually, but that doesn't sound as exciting - I came up with the answer. Just in time it transpired as the first of this year's carol-singers arrived tonight, later than usual as it happened as when the first of them arrived last year it was still November.

The doorbell rang right in the middle of Coronation Street when Sophie, or maybe it was Rosie, was having a go at Sally. I left her to it and answered the door. Four carol singers were without, although not without those Santa Claus hats beloved of bus drivers and football fans at this time of the year. I opened my mouth and began to sing –

Good King Wenceslas looked out
On the feast of Stephen
When the snow lay round about
Deep and crisp and even......

I sang the carol all the way through. Two of the carol singers looked at me throughout in something approaching awe. The other two eyed me as though they were looking at someone who should be in a rubber room at the happy farm.

I ended the carol and then held out my hand. Either going along with the flow or scared that I might attack him if he did otherwise, one of the ones who thought I was mad put his hand in his pocket, produced a pound coin and thrust it into my hand. I thanked him, wished he and his friends a very merry Christmas, closed the door on them and returned to the living room. Sophie, or maybe it was Rosie, was still having a go at Sally.

****

"Shall we go for a walk?" I said to The Trouble yesterday. "We usually do on New Year's Day."

She looked doubtfully through the window. "The weather looks a bit dodgy don't you think?"

She was right, it did look dodgy, the skies as murky and grey as an Afghan's underpants. But I fancied a walk and bravado had its usual victory over common sense. "No, I've seen it like this before," I said confidently. "I'm sure it won't rain for hours."

"I'll get my oilskin and sou'wester," said The Trouble, displaying her usual lack of faith in my judgment.

She didn't put on her oilskin and sou'wester, she hasn't got either, she was just being facetious, but she did put on waterproof clothing and Wellington boots. I should have done the same, but having said that the weather would remain fine I couldn't very well without looking face.

We set off walking on the nature trail. The trail used to be a railway line before Dr Beeching set about the country's railway system like Ghengis Khan on crack cocaine, is fairly straight and flat, and set as it is in picturesque surroundings it makes an excellent walk of about five miles there and back.

The surface, usually prone to be a bit muddy, had been newly laid with crushed limestone, It was being put to the test by quite a few youngsters who had obviously been given mountain bikes for Christmas. The 'in' colour this year for children's bikes would seem to be a sort of purple, which in a couple of instances matched the colour of the perspiring faces of the parents who were trying manfully to keep up with their offspring.

About fifty minutes later we arrived at the end of the trail and turned round to head back. We hadn't walked more than a hundred yards when the heavens opened.

"Probably just a shower," I said, more in hope than expectation.

The Trouble gave me a sweet smile, took her rain hat from her pocket and pulled it down over her head.

It rained every step of the way home. Poured. If Noah had still been around he would have started building another ark. The newly-laid crushed limestone very soon turned into, if not a quagmire, then at the very least a quag. Walking on it was like trying to walk through porridge, which it soon began to resemble.

On the way we met the returning bicycling families. Except that the parents had dismounted and were now not only pushing their cycles but those of their children. Little Brad and little Angelina were trailing some yards behind them either crying or moaning, often both.

I couldn't have been more wet if I'd jumped in the reservoir that borders part of the trail. Plus I was at least two stones heavier due to the fact that I was wearing a fleece, under which I had a woollen pullover. If there is anything more absorbent than a fleece and a woollen pullover it's a pair of denim jeans, which I was also wearing.

I don't know if anyone has ever calculated how much water a pair of jeans can soak up but if it's anything less than a bathful I'd be greatly surprised. The man who invents denim tampons will make a fortune. I can see the TV commercial now. 'Not only a super absorbent but also a fashion statement!'

Lugging two extra stones for two and a half miles whilst literally soaked to the skin is not to be recommended, especially when accompanied by someone relatively dry who keeps saying things like 'I told you I didn't like the look of the weather' and 'Well you should have worn your waterproofs' and 'The trouble with you is you don't listen'. So by the time I arrived home I was thoroughly pissed off as well as being thoroughly pissed on. Happy New Year!

****

January 14 2010. *BATS.*

I have had another BATS today. BATS is my acronym for Bloody Awful Telephone Salesperson. On a Saturday for God's sake! They usually have the grace to ring you up on a weekday even if they don't have the good sense not to ring you up when you've just that moment sat down to your evening meal or climbed into the bath, which they somehow always contrive to do. At least this one managed to pronounce my surname correctly. What I usually get, in a foreign accent that has its origins anywhere from the Mediterranean to Bangladesh, is: "Hello, is that Mr Ravenscroft" with the Raven part of my name pronounced 'ravern' as in 'cavern', and not, as it should be, 'raven' as in the bird. This is more often than not further mispronounced by leaving the 't' off the end and adding an 'f' in its place, to make 'Ravernscroff'. And I was once called, by a BATS who was probably a dyslexic Albanian, 'Ribscroff'. Whenever a BATS calls me the conversation usually goes something like this: -
ME: Hello?
BATS: Is that Mr Ravernscroff?
ME: No.

BATS: It isn't Mr Ravernscroff?

ME: No. It is Mr Ravenscroft.

BATS: I am doing a survey, Mr Ravernscroff, and I....

ME: (BUTTING IN) Call me back when you've learned how to pronounce my name properly.

Then I put the phone down. However on this occasion the BATS somehow managed to pronounce my name correctly, thus getting over the first hurdle and giving himself the chance to fall at the second, which he promptly did.

My ploy whenever a BATS successfully clears the first hurdle is to say "Hang on a minute will you there's someone at the door." Then I leave them hanging on the phone until it finally dawns on them I'm not coming back - anything from a couple of minutes to twenty or so, although I once had one supreme optimist hang on for an hour and a quarter - then, when they hang up and my phone starts making that awful noise it makes which tells you the line is still open, I too hang up. Sometimes, depending on how I'm feeling at the time, when I answer the phone I just say nothing and simply replace the receiver.

Occasionally I will let a BATS go on a bit, allowing him to think he has hooked me, before I deftly slip the bait, usually by telling him that thanks to his chatter I've allowed the chip pan to catch fire. And sometimes I pretend I am very hard of hearing so they have to shout so loud they're in great danger of straining their vocal chords. However the mood takes me.

As luck would have it when the BATS who called today rang - a rare Englishman - I was at a bit of a loose end, my usual Saturday afternoon at the football match having been called off due to a waterlogged pitch, so I allowed the call to go on for much longer than I normally would. Here is the gist of it -

BATS: Hello? Is that Mr Ravenscroft?

ME: Speaking.

BATS: We're doing a survey, I wonder if....

ME: Are you selling something?

BATS: No, we're just doing a survey.

ME: What about?

BATS: Food preparation in relation to cooking facilities.

ME: You're selling kitchens.

BATS: No, we're just doing a survey into....

ME: (BUTTING IN) Oh, shame. You see I'm in the market for a kitchen at the moment. But if you're not selling them I might as well hang up. Bye.

BATS: No! Don't hang up! I'm selling kitchens.

ME: Excellent. So then, how much are your kitchens? I'm not interested in anything cheap, mind. It's quality I'm looking for. The best.

BATS: The best?

ME: That's right, you've struck gold; you've hit the mother lode. So how much is your very best kitchen going to set me back?

BATS: Well our top of the range kitchen, in the average-sized home, with all appliances, would cost you, ball park (I let it go this time), about twenty two grand.

ME: I'll take two.

BATS: ....What did you say?

ME: I'll have two. You see my daughter lives next door and it's her twenty-first soon, I thought I'd surprise her. That's all right is it, you can do two?

BATS: Well, yes. Yes, of course.

ME: And when can you deliver?

165

BATS: Six weeks is the usual.

ME: Excellent. Have you got a pen, I'll give you my address.

BATS: I've got your address, 17 Lingland....

ME: No. That's my brother's address. Terry Ravenscroft. I'm Tom Ravenscroft, I'm staying with Terry at the moment. And my address is 27 Woologongong Springs, Brisbane, Queensland, Australia. Have you got that? Hello?....Hello?

****

February 14 2010. *COSMETICS.*

"Would you mind getting me a potato peeler, one of the French sort?" I said to the woman about to enter Boots. She looked me up and down with suspicion, probably wondering why I wasn't capable of getting it myself. "I suffer from Pharmophobia," I said by way of explanation, "A fear of chemists' shops."

Looking far from convinced the woman nevertheless took the five pound note I proffered.

"I may be some time," she warned, rather like a female version of Captain Oates but without the snowshoes and frostbite.

"Take all the time you want," I said, magnanimously.

Earlier on that morning The Trouble had said, "If you go anywhere near the precinct call in at Boots and pick me up a potato peeler, would you? One of the French type. I can't find mine anywhere."

"No problem," I assured her.

However there was a problem, but it had been so long since I'd been in Boots I'd forgotten all about it. The problem was, and is, that I find it hard to go in Boots without

166

bursting out laughing at the bizarre appearance of the assistants behind the cosmetics counter. And as the cosmetics counter is the first thing you encounter on entering a Boots you can't really miss it, and with it the grotesques lined up behind it. I don't know what time these creatures have to get up in the morning in order to put on their make-up in the lavish quantities they do but I would have thought that, unless they had the advantage of a plasterer's float, it would hardly be worth their while going to bed in the first place.

Atkins has the theory that as an incentive to maximise sales they are made to apply each morning any make-up not sold on the previous day, and he could be right.

One might think that in order to avoid collapsing in mirth on entering Boots I have only to keep my eyes to the front and ignore the cosmetics counter, but that's much easier said than done, because it seems to draw you. It's rather like being on a train seated opposite a pretty woman whose skirt has ridden up to reveal thighs and underwear - you try not to look but you just can't help yourself.

I was with The Trouble the first time I realised I had this problem. The assistant in question opened her mouth, a crimson gash that I can only liken to a pig with its throat cut. "Good morning madam, what can I get for you?" she smiled. She had to smile, she had no choice in the matter, she was wearing so much foundation cream and face powder that her face was set in a fixed grin. She would have been smiling if she'd said, "Good morning madam, a mad axe man is just about to bring his axe down on your head."

I didn't laugh at first, managing to contain myself to a barely-contained grin. It was when The Trouble noticed me grinning and said: "Take no notice of him he's got a feeble mind," that I started to laugh, aware that people with feeble minds can get away with anything and cashing in on it.

Ever since then I've kept out of Boots, confining myself to a quick look through the entrance every now and then confirm that the cosmetics counter staff still make me laugh, in the hope that they don't, as I'd quite like to go into Boots sometimes. However they still do.

Twenty minutes after she'd gone in the woman came out potato peeler-less and handed me back my five pound note. "They're sold out," she said, then, helpfully, "But they sell them at Debenhams, I bought one there a week or two ago."

I thanked her and trotted off to Debenhams. And I was actually in Debenhams before I realised that they, like Boots, have their cosmetics counter hard by the entrance. I saw the cosmetics assistants, clones of those at Boots. Naturally I laughed.

"Did you get that potato peeler?" said The Trouble, the moment I got in.

"They were sold out."

"Good. No matter, the other one turned up. Sorry to have wasted your time"

"That's all right," I replied. "Actually it was a bit of a laugh."

****

March 3 2010. *DRUG TRIP.*

My anal pain continues to plague me. It hasn't got any worse but then it hasn't got any better. It's a bit like having Jonathan Ross come to stay for a week - I could just about put up with it but I'd far rather do without it. I thought I'd tried everything in my efforts to rid myself of it, but no;

apparently there was hope in the shape of space cakes. Also in the space cakes, along with hope, was something else, for space cakes, I have since found to my cost, are chocolate brownies with the addition of a quantity of cannabis resin.

My nephew Glen suffers from multiple sclerosis and I had learned that he regularly takes doses of cannabis to ease the pain of this condition. I wondered if it would do the same for my anal pain and asked him. He confirmed what I had been told, highly recommended it and offered to furnish me a supply. Glen explained that he took the cannabis rolled up in cigarettes along with tobacco, a concoction known as a spliff I'm told, but I said I didn't want to do that as it took me ages to give up smoking and I didn't want to take the risk of it starting me off again. No problem, Glen would get his fair wife Lorna to bake me some space cakes. A couple of hours later I returned from Glen's with a brown paper bag containing eight of the so-named cakes.

The following day The Trouble had gone to visit her sister so I had the house to myself. Armed with the space cakes and the new David Lodge book I made myself comfortable on the settee. My favourite author's intelligent prose was very soon way beyond my comprehension, in fact I doubt very much if I could have managed to make sense of the 'Mr Men'.

I had asked Glen how many space cakes I would need to take. He advised that a certain amount of caution was required and that I should first try one, and if nothing happened have another one. I tried one. Nothing happened. I tried another. Whether something would have happened if I'd waited a little longer for the first space cake to work I will never know, but what I know for certain is that something definitely happened about two minutes after I'd eaten the second space cake.

It was a good job I was seated because the room suddenly started to go round and round. And kept on going round. Faster. For about two hours. I'd never wondered what it would be like to be in a spin-drier set on maximum but if I had that's what it would have been like. After about two minutes of the two hours the sound effects started up in the form of a big drum being beaten at about the rate of one beat every second. It was very loud but at the same time seemed far away and sort of hollow, ethereal, funereal even. After two more minutes I became totally consumed by abject fear. For the life of me I couldn't say what I was frightened about, either now or then. What I can say is that I was ten times more frightened than I've ever been in my life, and then some. Maybe it was the wallpaper that frightened me, previously an off-white with a light brown and green bamboo here and there, now purple and emerald stripes with orange stars here and there. I will never know.

And that was it for the next two hours, at which point I began to feel slightly better, inasmuch as I was then only scared shitless.

Throughout the two hours I had been absolutely, totally helpless. If someone had told me they would give me a million pounds if I raised one of my arms in the air I wouldn't have been able to do it. If someone had told me Kristin Scott Thomas was mine for the asking she would have remained unasked for. Whether or not the space cakes had done anything for my anal pain I have no idea, but very probably, as I'm pretty sure that if someone had hit me over the head with a lump hammer I wouldn't have felt a thing, let alone a pain in my bottom.

My mouth now began to feel dry. Within seconds later it was absolutely parched. The Gobi Desert isn't drier. I had to have a drink of water. I tried to stand up. I would have stood more chance trying to poke half a pound of butter up a hedgehog's arse with a red hot needle. After another fifteen minutes or so I just about managed to roll off the settee and onto my hands and knees. I don't know how long it took me to crawl from the living room into the kitchen but it seemed like two years.

I made my way to the sink and managed to drag myself up far enough to get my mouth under the tap and turn it on. I must have drunk at least a gallon of water before my thirst was quenched. I sank to my knees. It had now been over two hours since I'd had a pee, a long time for me, especially as I'd just drunk a gallon of water, and now I had to go to the toilet. I dragged myself up the stairs one at a time. I will skip the job I had having a pee after I eventually made it to the bathroom as it is far too embarrassing but a mop was later involved. When I'd finished I just sat there on the bathroom floor, not daring to go downstairs in case I had to go back up again.

It took the best part of five hours before I was anything like back to normal. I phoned Glen and told him what had happened. He just laughed and said that I'd slightly overdosed and been on a trip. It was a trip I will never be going on again and to make sure I didn't I threw the remaining space cakes in the bin. When The Trouble returned a bit later on I was sat on the settee reading my book. "I hope you haven't been sat there all day," she said.

"No, I had a trip out earlier," I said.

****

171

March 16 2010. *BREASTS.*

The Sunday Times TV listings tells me that on BBC 3 tonight there is a programme called 'My Breasts and I'. I thought at first it might be a new situation comedy, about the Breast Family, Joanne Breast, her thick husband George Breast, their children Jason and Samantha Breast who keep coming through doors and grinning like loonies, and their next-door neighbour Jeremy who is so thick that if he fell into a barrel of tits he'd climb out sucking his thumb; sort of like 'My Family' but with laughs. But no, apparently it is a documentary about female breasts.

The Sunday Times writes of it - 'More than you could possibly want to know about how the former Atomic Kitten Jenny Frost feels about her bosoms ('Two tea bags after they've been dunked', is how she sums them up). Plus how lots of other women (among them Joan Collins) feel about them, and a bra-fitting from the Queen's corsetiere (though not, as you might guess, with an appearance from the Queen)'.

I don't know the feelings of others on the subject but a glimpse of the Queen's breasts is not high on my list of things I am aching to see, so the news that we won't be seeing the royal nipples is by no means a disappointment. Having said that there is no reason to suppose that Elizabeth Regina's knockers might be, like Atomic Kitten Jenny Frost's, like two tea bags. On the contrary there is every reason to suppose that the Queen's breasts will be firm and pert, their nipples pointing outwards rather than at her feet; after all, her hairstyle hasn't altered since she was an eighteen-year-old so why should her breasts have changed? Her hair has changed colour of course, from brown to grey, so maybe she has grey breasts now, or breasts with grey hair on them, but I'd wager quite a bit that they're still the same shape.

I should of course know for a fact if the Queen's mammaries are the same shape, God knows there's been enough pictures of her in the newspapers and on television over the years to enable one to form an opinion, but since I was old enough to think for myself whenever I see a picture of the Queen in the newspapers I move quickly on to something less boring, without taking the trouble to examine the latest state of her breasts.

There is still an Atomic Kitten's tea bag tits to look forward to seeing though, in addition to those of Joan Collins, whose tits by now must also look like two tea bags, or if they don't it can only be because she's had them pumped full of silicone.

Thank Christ I won't have to watch it.

****

April 4 2010. *WHEELIE BINS.*

"I'd like a picture of a pizza." I said to the man at the pizza shop.

He frowned. "A picture of a pizza?"

I pointed to a picture of a pizza Napolitano on the wall. "That one would suit."

"You don't want a pizza?

I explained. "We only have one every couple of weeks or so and we had one last week. Very nice it was too. A Four Seasons with extra garlic. But today it's just a picture of one that I want. I'll quite willingly pay for it."

"Why do you want a picture of a pizza?"

173

I told him and five minutes later walked out with a rolled-up picture of the Napolitano under my arm, free of charge, and a bag of chips in my hand which I didn't really want but which I'd bought because the pizza man had been so nice about letting me have the picture for nothing.

About a couple of months ago the town council had delivered a green wheelie bin to my door, a companion for its black brother. With it came a list of things I could throw into it and which I would no longer be allowed to throw into the black bin. I would be given a month to get used to the new system of only throwing certain things in one bin and certain things in the other bin, thereafter if I put a certain thing in the wrong bin the bin men would refuse to empty it. There was no mention of uncertain things, such as something for the green bin which had become contaminated by something for the black bin, such as a shoe box with the remains of the Sunday dinner in it, but I suppose the council can't think of everything. There was also no mention as to how the bin men would know if someone ignored the new system and just carried on putting all their refuse in one or other of the bins and used the other bin as a mobile water butt or something. I asked.

"The refuse collection operatives have been instructed to look inside your bin from time to time," said the council official. "And in answer to your other question, who would be daft enough to put the remains of a Sunday dinner in a shoe box?"

"Me," I said. I paused, giving him the chance to apologise for calling me daft. No apology was forthcoming, so, pausing only to mount my high horse, I went on. "There was nothing daft about it. Both as a method of maximising available bin space and as a means of keeping the inside of

174

the wheelie bin free from encrusted food it was quite the reverse of daft, it was eminently sensible."

"Well it isn't eminently sensible any more, it is contravening our new refuse disposal guidelines," he said. I didn't argue with him. I know when I'm beaten.

One morning last week I answered the door to one of the bin men.

"There's a cardboard box in your black wheelie bin," he said.

I didn't argue with the bin man either. He was right, I realised as soon as he said it. A couple of nights previously The Trouble and I had dined on a takeaway pizza. Just as we were about to eat it a friend of The Trouble's brought round some home-made apple pie, still hot from the oven, and to do it justice we'd left a good half of the pizza, which I then threw into the bin along with the box.

"So we're not moving it," the bin man smirked.

It was the smirk that did it. If it hadn't been for that I would have put my hand up, maybe even apologised, offered to separate the pizza from the box, put them in their respective black and green bins and let the matter go. But there are certain things I won't stand for and one of them is public servants, whose wages are partly paid for by me, smirking at me.

Two days later me and the man from the council who had put me in my place made our way to my black wheelie bin.

"I can see how your refuse collection operative made the mistake," I said. "Especially as at that time in the morning the light wouldn't have been too good."

I swung back the lid of the wheelie bin. At the top of the assorted household rubbish was the pizza box. I had previously removed the pizza from it and in its place had put the picture of the pizza Napolitano kindly donated to me by the man at the pizza shop the day previously. "As you can see, he was wrong. Furthermore there was no need for him to take pleasure in informing me that I had transgressed your regulations and I insist that you to take him to task about it."

"I'll have a word with him," said the man from the council. "And please accept apologies.

The lengths you have to go in order to stay ahead of the game.

****

June 2 2010. *THE NEIGHBOURS FROM HELL.*

A month ago to the day the Pollitts moved into the house next-door-but-one that had been empty and up for sale for the last six months, following the death of its owner Mrs Linney. I didn't know immediately that the Pollitts were Neighbours from Hell, but early indications were that you wouldn't bet against it. That they arrived in an old off-road vehicle, the transport of choice of Neighbours from Hell in my experience, was a pointer I failed to note at the time.

There are five Pollitts in all, four if you ignore the baby, which Mr and Mrs Pollitt are obviously in the habit of doing as they left it crying for the entire three hours it took them to move in, after first securing it to an ornamental stone bird bath in the back garden. Two minutes later they tied their dog to the birdbath alongside the baby and thereafter it was a toss-up which of them was making the most noise.

Mr Pollitt's low forehead gives him a distinctly Neanderthal appearance. Low foreheads invariably indicate low intelligence whereas high foreheads indicate high

176

intelligence, and although either Ant or Dec - I'm not sure which, I've never been able to watch them for long enough to find out which is which, but the least short one - disproves the high forehead/high intelligence theory, I suspect that in Mr Pollitt's case it would stand up to the closest scrutiny.

Mrs Pollitt could best be described as a cross between Janice Battersby of Coronation Street and a pit bull terrier, but nowhere near as refined. She was wearing a sort of giant pink babygro, multi-coloured Wellington boots with flowers on and a facial expression like a smacked arse.

The boy is about fourteen, that magical age when a teenager goes from knowing hardly anything at all to knowing absolutely everything. He has no visible skin on his face so far as I can tell, the spaces between his acne and his tattoos being taken up by a collection of ironmongery consisting mainly of rings and metal studs.

The girl, at a guess a year younger, is at the age when a girl's periods arrive, along with a large helping of attitude. Her general demeanour indicated that she had recently taken delivery of these twin curses, the latter in spades. She wore a pair of green cycling shorts under a purple tutu and a crop top with the words 'Too Drunk to Fuck' written on the front.

The dog is of indeterminate ancestry. It certainly has some collie in it, although what was in the collie, or what the collie was in, isn't clear, possibly an Old English sheepdog or an Irish wolfhound. It is a sort of muddy grey, or mud and grey, its fur matted, and has two dreadlocks hanging down each side of its head.

Of the six of them the dog looks by some distance to be the most intelligent, but as even the most intelligent dog in the world would be incapable of fashioning its own dreadlocks it is obvious that one of the Pollitts must have

177

plaited them into its fur. And if they're capable of doing that what else are they capable of? I shuddered to think.

Mr Pollitt is called Wayne. His wife is not called Waynetta, although she might well be, but Liz. The boy is Keanu. The girl is Catherine Zeta. The baby has been blessed with the name Honey Nectarine. The dog is called You Twat, if Wayne Pollitt's instruction to it to 'Get from under the bleeding feet you twat,' and Catherine Zeta Pollitt's 'Stop trying to shag my fucking leg you twat' are anything to go by.

Judging by their accents Pollitt is probably from Manchester, his wife from London, the kids from Hell. I didn't have to ask their names. They could be heard clearly by anyone within half a mile of their back garden, even the deaf. The dialogue went something like:-

Wayne Pollitt: "Liz, for fuck's sake give Honey Nectarine her fucking dummy."

Liz Pollitt: "I'm tryin' to wean 'er off it ain't I."

Catherine Zeta Pollitt: "Keanu's just fumped me again, Mum!"

Keanu Pollitt: "Well she were tickling t' dog's bollocks."

Catherine Zeta Pollitt: "He likes 'avin' his bollocks tickled."

Liz Pollitt: "All males do, Caffrin Zee-ah, all males do."

Keanu Pollitt: "The slag already knows that."

Catherine Zeta Pollitt: "Fuck off you!"

Etc. Mercifully they all went out in their yobmobile in the afternoon. Except for the dog that is, which spent half the afternoon in the back garden, barking. The other half it spent howling.

I could see the dog, tied to a clothes-line pole, from our back bedroom window. In an effort to shut it up I opened the window, took a small ornament we could do without from the window bottom and threw it at it. My hope was that even if I missed the dog it might take it as a warning and stop barking in case the next one hit it, or if it did hit it give it something to bark about. It landed about a yard away. The dog ate it. Or at least it attempted to eat it, before spitting it out in disgust. Then it carried on alternately barking and howling until the Pollitts returned.

The following day all the Pollitts went out early; Wayne Pollitt and his wife Liz presumably to work, Keanu and Catherine Zeta to school, or more likely to hang about the local shopping arcade possibly dealing drugs; the baby, Honey Nectarine, probably to a childminder, or maybe a kennels. The dog was not placed in kennels and was left out in the garden to howl and bark like a demented Dervish all day.

I could see the way things were going so I wasted no time in reporting the situation to the Environmental Health people, who promised to send someone round. However if I knew them it would be in their own good time, so what to do about it in the meantime? I write my books every morning for three or four hours - I was into the last couple of chapters of 'Inflatable Hugh' at the time - and I wasn't going to be able to write a word with that racket going on. Perhaps if I were to sneak up on the dog armed with the carving knife and cut off its dreadlocks it would get the message, much as Delilah had quietened down Samson when she cut off his hair? A nice thought, but improbable. Far better to cut off its testicles with the carving knife; there would be more and louder howling initially but it wouldn't last for long. In the end I decided to take a less direct, more diplomatic route, and reason with the Pollitts, so when they had all returned to their lair that evening I called round.

Pollitt answered the door, surliness personified. "What?"

"I'm your next-door-but-one neighbour. It's about your dog."

At this his bottom lip jutted out even further. "What about it?"

"It's been in your back garden all day long barking and howling."

He cocked an ear. "I can't hear anything."

"That could be because it isn't barking and howling now. Possibly because you've fed it."

"Nobody else has complained."

"That's because everyone else goes out to work during the day. They wouldn't be able to hear it while they're a work. Unless they're unfortunate enough to work within a five mile radius of your back garden. Anyway I want you to put a stop to it."

"And how am I supposed to do that?"

"Well one way would be to keep it in the house, not out in the back garden.

"If we do that it shits in the house."

"Well train it to shit somewhere else."

"We have, we've trained it to shit in the garden."

"But if you leave it in the garden it barks and howls all day. Probably because it's up the arse in shit. But whatever the reason it's not good enough and I insist you put a stop to it."

"Tell him to fuck off and mind his own fucking business, Dad." Catherine Zeta had joined her father. She turned her attention to me, and reiterated her advice, lest her father hadn't heard her. "Fuck off and mind your own fucking business."

"You heard the little lady," said Pollitt, and closed the door in my face.

I rang the Environmental Health people and reported the conversation. The man there said he had every sympathy but it would take about three months to deal with. "Initial letter. Follow up letter in stronger terms when they ignore the initial letter. Then, if they ignore the letter in stronger terms, a letter threatening them with County Court." I congratulated him and his department for pulling out all the stops. Without a trace of irony in his voice he thanked me for my kind words and said they were only doing their job. I told Atkins about the situation with the dog and he offered to shoot it for me. I was tempted but told him I wasn't that desperate yet.

The following day, having paced out the distance from the end of my house to the middle of the Pollitt's house, I found that the nearest point of our back garden to the clothes-line post to which the Pollitt's dog is tethered to be 26 yards. I estimated that the chain by which the dog is hitched to the clothes-line post to be eight feet in length. This meant that I would have to throw an eight ounce minced-beef and crushed-sleeping pills ball a distance of 26 yards and land it in a sixteen feet diameter circle. A piece of cake. Or rather a piece of minced-beef and crushed- sleeping pill.

The Trouble came into the kitchen "Why are you making meatballs?"

"They're for the Pollitt's dog."

"You're going to try feeding it? In the hope it will stop barking?"

"In the certain knowledge it will stop barking."

181

I put The Trouble in the picture as I added the six crushed sleeping pills to the pound of beef mince and formed it into two eight ounce balls. I half-expected her to raise some opposition to my plan as she used to be in the RSPCA until the day she swerved to miss a cat and suffered a whiplash injury and went off animals, but none came. No doubt she was as heartily sick and fed up with the Pollitt's dog barking and howling as I was. "Right," I said, "get yourself upstairs and watch out of the back bedroom window and tell me if I hit the target."

"Aren't you going to cook the meatballs first?"

"No, they might disintegrate in flight if I cook them."

Her latent RSPCA connection emerged. "You'll give the dog worms, feeding it raw meat."

"That won't worry it, it'll be asleep. I shouldn't think the worms will be too active either."

The Trouble went up to the bedroom and I went out into the back garden. The dog was howling fit to burst. I'd already been down to the park for half-an-hour's practice to get my range - no sign of the Zimmer Frame team practicing so they might by now have abandoned the idea - but even so I decided to take the precaution of having a practice throw in situ with a large pebble the same weight as the meat ball. I took up my position and tossed the pebble into the Pollitt's garden. The howling increased.

"You've hit the dog," said The Trouble, from the bedroom window.

"Good." Having found my range I then expertly tossed the first of the meatballs. The barking stopped. I looked up to The Trouble. "Did it land in the target area?"

"Yes."

"What's happening? Is the dog eating it?"

182

"It's sniffing at it."

I waited a moment or two. "Well?"

"It's still sniffing at….no, no it's turned its nose up at it; it's turned away."

"Shit!"

"I said you should have cooked it, the trouble with you is you don't listen."

I had to admit she could be right. After all the meat in tins of dog food is cooked. I decided to leave things as they were for the time being in the hope the dog would change its mind and eat it. If it didn't I would have another go with a cooked meatball at the next available opportunity. The barking continued until the Pollitts arrived home so it looked like the dog had continued to ignore the meatball, either that or it ate it and it's got a stronger constitution than I'd given it credit for.

After cooking the second of the spiked meatballs, in fact deliberately overcooking it in an effort to make it as solid as possible and thus less prone to disintegrating in flight like one of Barnes Wallis's early attempts at the Bouncing Bomb, and after allowing it to cool down sufficiently, I took it out into the garden and prepared to propel it into the Pollitt's back garden.

The Trouble was out so this time I had to manage without her assistance, but as this also meant managing without her criticism I wasn't too put out about it. Once again I tossed a trial pebble before unleashing the meatball. On Friday the pebble had hit the dog. Unfortunately this time it didn't, leastwise the dog didn't start howling any louder. Confident I'd judged the distance correctly I quickly followed the pebble with the meatball. By the time I'd gone upstairs to check on the result the dog was champing away hungrily on the meatball. I looked on in the certain knowledge that it would soon be taking forty winks, or more likely four hundred winks, and that I'd soon be able to enjoy a bit of peace and quiet again and get on with Inflatable Hugh. I got my binoculars out to get a better sight of the beast departing for the Land of Nod. However, as well as the dog my binoculars picked out something on the ground nearby. At first I thought it was a large dog turd but then recognised it as the raw meatball I'd thrown the day before. It had been there all day without any of the Pollitts noticing it, or more likely noticing it and wrongly identifying it as just another of the dog's multitude of turds, as I had. Having finished the meatball the dog stood there salivating and licking its lips. Then, no doubt having acquired a taste for beef mince meatballs it set about eating the previously ignored raw meatball. Making it a dozen sleeping pills it had swallowed. Having quickly polished that off as well the dog stood smacking its chops and looking around hopefully for another meatball.

Once the dozen sleeping pills had kicked in I expected it to start getting drowsy, and maybe stagger about drunkenly for a bit before giving up the ghost, lying down, and going to sleep, but no, after about thirty seconds it simply dropped to the ground like a stone. There was a single violent twitch from its hind legs as it rolled over onto its back, then no further movement, not so much as a flicker. I watched it for a good ten minutes and it didn't move a muscle. It looked as dead as a doornail to me, which could very well have been the case after swallowing a dozen sleeping pills all at one go. It's certainly quietened it down though.

It was still in exactly the same position when I looked again about six-o-clock. The Pollitts had all arrived home by

184

this time but none had apparently noticed the lack of life in the dog; either that or they'd noticed and didn't give a toss. Probably the latter.

The following day I answered the door to an angry-looking Wayne Pollitt.

"What do you know about what happened to our fucking dog?" he demanded.

I am an accomplished liar when the occasion demands, especially when faced with an irate man big enough to eat me for breakfast I, so I feigned complete innocence. "Has something happened to your dog?" I said, a picture of neighbourly concern.

"It's been asleep since yesterday and all day today. The vet says it's in a fucking."

"I see." I thought for a moment, as if addressing myself to the problem of bringing the dog out of its coma. "You could try singing to it."

"What?"

"What's its favourite piece of music? 'How Much is that Doggy in the Window' perhaps?" I searched my brain for other dog songs. "'Old Shep' maybe?"

His bloodshot eyes bore into me. "Are you fucking mental?"

"Not at all. It's a proven fact that if you play their favourite pieces of music to people in a coma it quite often brings them back to consciousness. There was a case in the papers only the other week. A couple constantly played James Blunt songs to their mother and she came out of the coma after three days. Mind you it put the couple and one of the nurses *into* a coma but....And if it works for people there's no reason why it shouldn't work for dogs."

185

Pollitt eyed me balefully. "Anyway, what do you know about what happened to it, Mr Clever fucker?"

I remained cool. "What makes you think I know anything about it?"

"Because you're the twat what complained about it, aren't you."

"I regularly complain to the window cleaner that he's missing the corners but I've never yet felt the need to put him into a coma for it."

He made a fist and brandished it under my nose. "If I find out it was you had anything to do with it I'll fucking well chin you."

"Very well. But you won't. Have a nice day."

The following day brought good news and even better news. The good news was that the Pollitt's dog had finally come out of its coma. Whether this had anything to with Wayne Pollitt or any of his clan singing 'How Much is that Doggy in the Window' or 'Old Shep' into its earhole isn't clear; probably not. More likely it was one of the other methods the Pollitts usually employ to stir it into action, such as kicking it or tickling its testicles, which brought it back to the land of the living. (The reader might be surprised to learn that I consider the dog's return to consciousness as good news. However, although an intolerant man when it comes to dogs barking I am not an evil or vindictive person, and I certainly didn't want the dog to die. Granted I could have done with it staying in a coma for a little longer - about five years would have been nice - but then I'm only human.)

The even better news is that the dog spent all day in the back garden, with all the Pollitts out of the house, and didn't bark once. Perhaps, after its traumatic experience, it was simply taking time to build up its energies before returning to full barking and howling mode, but hopefully not. Maybe due to its enforced sleep something has happened to it psychologically, and it now felt it could get by without having to bark and howl its fool head off all day. I couldn't even induce it to bark. In an effort to do this I lobbed several small rocks and half a red brick at it and although they didn't hit it some of them landed quite close, but if it noticed them it didn't give any indication, and made not so much as a murmur.

Whilst I was doing this Atkins called round and when I'd explained to him what I was trying to achieve he offered to return home and get his shotgun to see if both barrels of shot in the dog's behind would get it barking again. I thanked him for the offer but told him that both barrels of shot in the dog's behind would almost certainly not only get it barking again but keep it barking for a very long time, and that was the last thing I wanted. Atkins said that if this happened he also had a .303 Lee Enfield rifle amongst his arsenal of weapons and could quickly and humanely put the dog out of its misery. I thanked him and put Atkins's suggestion on the back burner.

It made a move towards the front burner the following morning when the dog started barking again. It wasn't barking very often, it must be admitted, and only for short spells and in a very muted manner, and it still hadn't started howling again, but I felt sure it was only a matter of time before it would be at it again.

The Trouble said, "You know what's wrong with that dog, don't you?"

"Yes," I replied. "What's wrong with it is that I only gave it a dozen sleeping pills instead of two dozen and a drop or two of cyanide and a space cake for good measure."

187

"What's wrong with it," she went on, ignoring my opinion in favour of her own, as usual, "is that no one ever takes it out for a walk. Barking is its way of drawing attention to itself, in the hope that someone will get the message and take it out for a walk."

I chewed on this. She was probably right. A daily walk might indeed quieten the brute down a little if not silence it altogether. A bullet would achieve the same object and with more certainly but....

The Trouble interrupted my thoughts. "Why don't *you* take it a walk?"

"Me?"

"Well it's you who's doing all the complaining. And I don't imagine that any of the Pollitts are ever going to take it for a walk."

I mulled over the idea for the rest of the day. The following morning I decided to take The Trouble's advice. I go for a walk every day as a matter of course so it wouldn't be as if I was putting myself to any inconvenience.

I'm pretty good with dogs and didn't anticipate any problems. I didn't get any at first. When I went through the gate and into the Pollitt's garden the dog stopped barking immediately and started wagging its tail. I went up to it, patted it on the head and stroked it a couple of times to show it I was friendly. So far so good. I then attached the piece of rope I'd brought with me in lieu of a lead to its collar. It was then that things started to go pear-shaped as the moment I did this it set off for the garden gate at a speed that would have left the Road Runner coming in a poor second.

I could probably have coped with a road runner but this was a big strong dog and as I held on to the rope its breaking strain was tested to the full and not found wanting.

Consequently my arm was almost wrenched out of its socket and both my feet left the ground at the same time. I was now on my knees, being dragged along the Pollitt's lawn towards the gate. I managed to stagger to my feet only just in time to avoid being dragged into the ornamental stone bird bath, and was dragged instead into a fully-laden clothes drying carousel, where my head became entangled in the washing lines. Fortunately I managed to grab hold of the carousel's central column with my spare hand otherwise my head could very well have been pulled clean off my shoulders.

The dog ploughed on regardless of my plight. Fortunately the carousel couldn't have been mounted very securely as after only token resistance the dog, assisted by me, pulled it clean out of the ground. I was now being dragged along the lawn again in a melee of carousel and Pollitt's sundry clothing.

Why I didn't let go of the lead the moment the dog took off I have no idea. Why didn't the bricklayer in Gerard Hoffnung's famous 'The Bricklayers Lament' let go of the rope when the barrel of bricks lifted him off his feet? Indeed why didn't Atkins let go of the lasso when the goose attacked him on the canal? I distinctly remember having to shout to Atkins "Let go of the rope you bloody fool!" before he was inspired to take this rather obvious action. All I can think of is that it must be something instinctive that takes over from rational thought when danger threatens, the natural inclination being to hang on to something rather than let go of it.

After common sense had eventually prevailed and I let go of the rope I hauled myself to my feet and took stock of myself. My right arm felt as though it had had a tug-of-war team pulling on it for the last half hour; my neck was

189

throbbing from being almost strangled; thanks to my unnatural exertions my bad back had started up again; and I was covered from head to foot in dog shit.

The dog stood at the back gate looking anxiously at me and wagging his tail. It could have wagged it until the cows came home as far as I was concerned. My dog-walking days were over; enough was enough.

As if my injuries weren't bad enough my pain was made even harder to bear the following day when the Pollitt's simply upped and left, just as quickly as they had arrived. I later found out that they'd only been renting the place for a month, or rather the council had been renting it for them whilst their council house was being redecorated after one of Catherine Zeta Pollitt's birthday party guests had torched a gatecrasher and set the house on fire.

****

October 1 2010. *VIAGRA.*

I saw on the television news this evening an item about baby Lewis Goodfellow, who weighed only 1lb 8ozs when he was born sixteen weeks premature last September with seriously underdeveloped lungs, and was given Viagra to treat this condition. Noting that seriously underdeveloped lungs would seem to be a desirable quality in a new born baby, if the nocturnal howlings my own three offspring when they were babies were anything to go by, and that it might be not a bad idea to keep the Viagra pills as far away from baby Lewis as possible, I watched the rest of the news item. It informed me that the prescribed male impotence drug worked by opening some of the small blood vessels in baby Lewis's lungs to help carry oxygen around the little mite's body. Now, six months later, he is finally at home with his delighted parents.

I myself can testify to the benefits of Viagra and I couldn't help wondering if as well as opening the blood vessels in little Lewis's lungs it had also done for him what it does for me. Less than a year old and able to get an erection, eh; he's going to be a little terror when he starts playschool.

It reminded me of Arthur Simmons, a classmate of mine when I was at infants school. Until the Viagra-fuelled Lewis Goodfellow came along Arthur, at nine and a bit, was by far the youngest person I had ever heard of who was able to achieve tumescence. All his classmates, me included, had to wait about another five years before we were presented with this wonderful gift. Not Arthur. He could get an erection at will. He could also get one without will, which he very often did, causing much merriment for his classmates and much embarrassment to Arthur. He shared a desk with Maisie Marshall and her hand would shoot up. "Miss, Miss, Arthur Simmons has got that lump in his trousers again."

Poor Miss Snotrag (her real surname was Gartons but one day Billy Higginbottom discovered that Snotrag was Gartons spelt backwards so she was Miss Snotrag from that moment until the day she retired), her face beetroot red, always tried to ignore the problem. "Get on with your composition about what you did during the Easter holidays, Maisie."

Maisie however was undeterred "My mam says it must be because he plays with his willy, Miss."

Now it was Arthur's turn to blush. "Don't Miss! Just happens." And it did. Often. In fact I think he spent more time with a hard on than with a hard off.

191

When out of the classroom and away from the girls - usually in the boys lavatories or down the old school air raid shelters - he wasn't anywhere near so bashful about his gift, and would get out his proud penis for the rest of us to gaze at in awe on request, and often without request. His penis wasn't very long - about four inches I would say - but as that was about three inches more than what the rest of we nine-year-olds had it was well worth looking at.

He could ejaculate as well. However at first he didn't know he could ejaculate, and the first time it happened he hadn't got a clue what was happening and apparently - unfortunately I didn't see it but I have it on very good authority - he thought he was erupting like Vesuvius and tried to stuff the semen back down his urethra. When it wouldn't go down and he'd stopped coming he wiped his hands on his trousers. Miss Snotrag told the inquisitive Maisie Marshall it was wallpaper paste and sent him home to change.

Needless to say all the boys in the class were very jealous of Arthur and his erection. A further cause of our envy was that he was excused Religious Instruction as the teacher, Mrs Dawlish, refused to have him and his tumescence in her class.

By the time we were eleven Arthur's erection had grown another inch but I don't know how it progressed from then on as at that age we went our separate ways, Arthur to the local secondary modern school, me, having passed the eleven plus, to the grammar school. I did see him occasionally, although not his penis, when I went shopping for my mother, as he helped out on Saturday mornings at the Co-op butchers, but we both felt it was inconvenient - and possibly dangerous given all the sharp knives and meat

192

cleavers being wielded in close proximity - for him to get it out in the shop.

I like to think that Arthur, having failed the eleven plus, one day reached this mark with his erection, but by the time we'd reached maturity he'd moved away, and I lost touch with him altogether, so sadly I will probably never know.

****

November 10 2010. *ELECTORAL ROLL.*

I answered the front door. I didn't like the look of the man who was stood there one little bit. He was wearing tinted glasses and I've always been suspicious about people who adopt this affectation ever since I saw that planet-saving pop singer, what's-his-name, Bongo or something, wearing them. Plus the man was carrying a briefcase, which almost certainly meant he would be either poking his nose into my business or trying to sell me something, both of which I could well do without.

"Mr Ravenscroft?" he said, in a tone of voice that in addition to incorporating a question mark also contained an unhealthy degree of hubris.

I ignored the question mark and went to work on the hubris by treating his statement as though it were an announcement. "Well what a coincidence! That's my name too. We must be related. Tell me, are you, like me, one of the Derbyshire Ravenscrofts? Or maybe you're one of the Scottish branch of the family?"

When confronted by arrogant people it has always been my policy to try to disrupt them right at the outset, to try to get them off the front foot and firmly on the back. I succeeded in this instance because for a few seconds the man

193

just stood there looking at me open-mouthed. Then he managed to close his mouth and another few seconds later started forming words with it. "No. You misunderstand. *I'm* not Mr Ravenscroft."

I affected surprise. "I thought you said you were?"

"No. I was enquiring if *you* were Mr Ravenscroft."

"Ah. I see. So then, now we've got that established (and that the arrogance has disappeared from your tone), what can I do for you?"

"It's about your Electoral Roll form."

"Yes? What about it?"

"Apparently we've sent you three and on each occasion you have failed to do the necessary."

"Wrong. I returned all three of them."

"Yes but you didn't fill them in and sign them."

"Right. That's because by the time I was old enough to vote I was old enough to realise that I don't wish to have an electoral role as the only thing politicians are interested in, having been elected Members of Parliament or town councillors, is feathering their own nest. My wife shares my views so she also wishes to have no role in any elections.

He looked at me as if to say "You stupid bugger." Unfortunately for him he isn't allowed to call me a stupid bugger, so instead he said, a leer now on his face and the hubris making a speedy comeback appearance, "It's not an Electoral Role R..O..L..E it's an Electoral Roll R..O..L..L, it's nothing to do with you having a 'role' in elections, nor your desire to vote or otherwise."

I stuck to my guns.

"Electoral….elector…elections….seems to me it has everything to do with voting and nothing to do with anything else."

"It is to do with the Local Authority knowing who precisely resides at every address within the boundaries of that Local Authority," he said, the voice of authority, or maybe the voice of local authority.

"You already know who lives here. My wife and me. You printed our names on the Electoral Roll forms under 'Names of People Living at this Address'."

"We need you to confirm it."

"Right, I confirm it. We live here."

"By signing the Electoral Roll form."

"Sorry, no can do. I sent them back. All three of them."

"I know." He treated me to a supercilious smile before opening his briefcase and producing a form. "I've brought along another one."

I took it off him, gave it a cursory examination then said: "Yes well it all seems to be in order, I'll sign it then. Shan't be a moment I'll get my pen."

I closed the door on him, put on a top coat and went out the back door for a walk. I don't know how long the man waited on the doorstep but he wasn't there when I returned about an hour later. He'll be back again I suppose, and I'll probably have to sign the Electoral Roll form next time. Donald Duck, I think. Or maybe Eric Cartman.

****

January 15 2010. *NUCLEAR FREE.*

The city of Manchester, which is only fourteen miles from my home town, just thirty minutes on the train on a good day, God knows how long on a bad, is a place I only ever visit out of absolute necessity. If I needed something and the only two places I could get it were Manchester and Siberia I would probably have to apply for a Siberian visa and check out the condition of my thermal underwear. That is not to say that Manchester is without its pockets of charm – King Street and the Castlefield area, with its concert hall and fine museums, are excellent - but these oasis are more than outweighed by its abundance of rubbish-strewn streets, grubby buildings and probably more Big Issue sellers to the square yard than anywhere else in England. However, needs must, and I had to visit it yesterday; and because of that visit I shall be visiting it again at least one more time, and when I do it will be because I want to, eagerly, and in a hell of a hurry.

Why has Manchester, once a city of dark satanic mills, now a city of dark satanic gay bars, suddenly become so attractive to me? Simply because quite by accident I have discovered that it is safe from nuclear attack, a haven from any future holocaust. Really? Well it is according to the official City of Manchester Council notice I saw on my way from Piccadilly station to House of Fraser on Deansgate. 'Welcome to Manchester,' the notice proclaimed, 'A nuclear free city'. That's for me, I thought, the first sign of World War Three breaking out and it's me, The Trouble, my children and my grandchildren Manchester bound, to stay there until the nuclear winter is over and it's safe to come out.

I don't quite know how being a nuclear free city works – however I'm sure the City of Manchester Council will have worked out something with the Russians - probably there'll be some sort of sensor in the nuclear missiles UK-bound and when they lock in on a plethora of Big Issue sellers they'll pass over; or more likely when their sensor homes in on the 'Welcome to Manchester, a nuclear free city' sign the missile will say to itself , "Ah, a nuclear free city, I mustn't transform it into a wasteland where nothing will be able to live for the next fifty years", then continue on and lay to waste the next place it comes to that isn't a nuclear free city, possibly Stockport. I hope so because I dislike Stockport even more than I dislike Manchester. Check, more than I did dislike Manchester. Because I've taken quite a shine to the old place now.

****

February 1 2010. *PINK.*

It's not every day you get the answer to something that's been puzzling you for years but today was one of them. And all I had to do was ask The Trouble.

Whilst shopping in Buxton this morning I had noticed a pink car. I've seen cars before that were pink on the outside and cars that were pink on the inside but this car was unusual in that it was pink on both the outside *and* the inside. The seats were bedecked in pink covers, the steering wheel wore a fluffy pink glove, a giant pair of pale pink dice with deep pink spots hung in the windscreen and a pink nodding dog sat stupidly in the back window awaiting nodding duties.

A notice in the rear window, 'Babe on Board', informed me that the car's owner was a female, unless there was a man who called himself 'Babe' who owned a totally pink car, which I very much doubted, unless Julian Clary was in town. This was confirmed a moment or two later when a blonde woman aged about twenty-five, dressed in a pink jump suit, walked out of the door of a hairdressers shop and made for the car. In addition to the pink jumpsuit she wore pink trainers, a pink ski cap and she was clutching a pink bag, which was no doubt filled with pink objects, purse, mobile phone, tissues, lipstick, vibrator, etc.

When this pink vision got in the car she virtually disappeared from sight, lost in all the pinkness. All you could see was a face and a pair of hands, seemingly floating in a sea of pink.

Years ago there used to be a company called 'The Black Theatre of Prague' who appeared on TV regularly, and whose act consisted of prancing about against a black background whilst wearing black jumpsuits and white gloves. All the viewer could see were disengaged pairs of hands seemingly floating about in the ether. Quite obviously this woman was 'The Pink Theatre of Buxton'.

It got me thinking about the thing that's been intriguing me for years, which is of course 'Why do women love pink so much?' I used to think it was because babies are pink and all women love babies, so by extension loving pink comes naturally to them. But then it dawned on me that women's breasts are pink and all men love women's breasts and men don't love pink, so....

"Why do all women like pink?" I asked The Trouble when I got home.

"That grid in the backyard is blocked again, you were supposed to be clearing it and all you can do is wonder why women wear pink?" she replied, quite sharply.

"I'll do it just as soon as I've found out why it is that women like pink," I said.

"It's so that men don't have to wear it," she said. "Now go and clear that grid. "

I went to clear the grid, a wiser man.

****

MARCH 1 2011. *A TIN OF PEAS.*

"Why are you sat holding a tin of peas to your arm?" I said, not unreasonably, to The Trouble, on entering the living room and discovering her in this bizarre pose. She gave me her frostiest look, which is pretty frosty; penguin's toes have been known to drop off when subjected to less frosty looks.

"You've no idea?" she asked.

I thought about it for a moment. "You've lost it? You couldn't find a tin of carrots? We've had the gas cut off and you're warming them through with the heat of your body? Any of those things perhaps?"

"Do you remember me asking you to bring a bag of frozen peas in with you from the corner shop?"

"I do. But as I've already explained to you, Mr Ahmed had run out. Had a run on frozen pea curry probably, so I got a tin of peas instead. The very tin you are now holding to your arm, my precious sweet marrowfat, unless I'm very much mistaken."

"And you think that will work, do you?"

"Work? What do you mean, work?"

"I knew you hadn't been listening properly. The trouble with you, Terence, is that you never do when I'm talking to you."

"Rubbish."

"You don't. If you'd been listening properly you'd have known I wanted the bag of frozen peas to hold to my arm to help reduce the swelling caused when I strained my bicep yesterday. In which case you wouldn't, on discovering that Mr Ahmed was out of frozen peas, have bought a tin of bloody peas instead!"

"....Yes I would," I replied calmly, after only a moment's hesitation while I struggled to come up with some excuse. "That's why I bought it."

"What?" This said with utter disbelief. That made two of us who didn't believe it but I had to say something.

"That's why I got the tin of peas instead," I said, managing to maintain a degree of smoothness that Rex Harrison would have been proud of.

The Trouble shook her head as if to clear it. "Am I missing something here?"

"Yes. You're missing the knowledge that it is a well known fact that holding a tin of marrowfat peas to a ruptured bicep is a sure-fire way of bringing the swelling down. Florence Nightingale swore by it."

The Trouble was immediately apologetic. "And there was I thinking I was being sarcastic," she said sheepishly.

"Is it working?" I inquired solicitously. "Has it brought the swelling down any yet?"

She drew back her arm and threw the tin of peas at me. She yelped out loudly in distress, the act of throwing the tin obviously causing her great pain in her strained muscle. I yelped out even more loudly as the tin caught me a nasty crack on the knee. In no time it became swollen. The Trouble suggested I should hold a tin of peas to it to bring down the swelling. She's getting as bad as I am.

****

March 9 2011. *THE END.*

It is my birthday today. I am 70. It is five years since I started writing this journal so it is mission accomplished. And guess what? I don't feel a day older. I feel five years older. But as I only felt 27 when I was 65 that's still only makes me 32, still in my prime. I am still reasonably fit, notwithstanding all the ailments I have mentioned within these pages, and I still don't need a stairlift. But I am a little nearer to one.

****

More books by Terry Ravenscroft

CAPTAIN'S DAY

At Sunnymere Golf Club meticulous plans put in place by club captain Henry Fridlington and his good lady wife Millicent ought to have guaranteed that his Captain's Day would be the best day of his life. However Henry has recently enforced a strict 'no swearing on the golf course' policy, a policy which has not gone down at all well with the membership - and a policy which is largely instrumental, along with more than a little help from Henry himself, in ensuring that far from being the best day of his life his Captain's Day turns into the very worst day of his life.

Better than sex - Lee Westwood
Not as good as sex - Tiger Woods

Reader's review:- *Having just read Stairlift to Heaven I was keen on more of Mr. Ravenscroft's output so I bought this little gem. It has a vague hint of Tom Sharpe about it, but much more accessible and I have to say probably much funnier. The whole book is based upon one day - the Captains Day at the golf course and has a cast of characters that many will know, even non-golfers.* M. G. Chisholm.

****

JAMES BLOND - STOCKPORT IS TOO MUCH

After foiling the plans of countless power-hungry villains bent on world domination the bringing to book of the evil Dr Goldnojaws, who only wants to dominate humble Stockport, England, shouldn't present too much of a problem for top secret agent James Blond. However in addition to taking on Goldnojaws and his evil sidekick BloJob, Blond has to wrestle with a prostate problem, so things aren't quite as straightforward as he would have liked. Then to make matters worse he starts having girlfriend trouble....with Pisa Vass, Divine Bottom, Gloria Snockers and Ava Shag amongst others. James Bond as you have never known him.

Reader's review:- *With James Blond - Stockport is Not Enough Terry Ravenscroft has penned another comedy winner. A clever and well written parody on Fleming's James Bond series, the parallels are nicely drawn whilst the story works equally well as a stand-alone piece. The humour is plentiful and down-to-earth without being overtly crude. Ravenscroft's prose, in this book as well as his others, is easy on the eye and sweeps the reader along at a pleasant and satisfying pace. There's never a dull moment but the action is never frenetic.* Tim Stevens.

****

INFLATABLE HUGH

We couldn't be meeting The Right Hon Hugh Pugh, MP, Secretary of State for Transport, at a worse time. A general election is only months away and it's a racing certainty that following it he will be out of a job. As things stand he can only just keep his head above water on his ministerial income, plus what he's still able to fiddle on expenses; with maintenance payments to make to three ex-wives, three of his children at private schools, and the latest in a string of high-maintenance girlfriends to keep fed, shod and watered, his future doesn't even bear thinking about. But then fate takes a hand when he inherits his late brother's inflatable rubber woman factory.

Reader's review:- *Apparently your brother maintained the belief that having sex with an inflatable rubber woman was almost as beneficial in creating a feeling of well-being as the real thing. This being the case he viewed his operation more like a public service than a moneymaking operation. Which isn't to say he didn't make substantial profits from the sales ..."*
Pugh's heart beat faster. Substantial profits. What a wonderful coming together of words.

With the above opening paragraph of Inflatable Hugh I was hooked. Terry Ravenscroft's tongue in cheek writing had me laughing out loud from beginning to end. From the wily to the ingenuous, from the morally

indignant Vigilantes Against Sex Toys to the crafty
machinations of politicians, all are depicted with subtle
insight into character. In recommending this as a
`great' read I could only paraphrase the author's own
writing: What a delightful coming together of words!
Rue.

****

DEAR AIR 2000

Letters from the world's most troublesome (some would
say troubled!) passenger. Dear Air 2000 is a hilarious
collection of correspondence to and from forty different
airline companies. After reading this book it is doubtful
if you will ever risk eating an airline lasagne ever again.
Over 100,000 copies already sold in paperback and
ebook.

Reader's review:- *Quickly nurse, the screens! More*
fabulous Terry Ravenscroft, best not read on the 295
bus to Clapham Station as you will get funny looks
trying to hold in the laughter and tears. I can't comment
if it would be any better on the C1 bus as it never seems
to turn up. Dear Air 2000 is just a joy to read. There
are some slightly saucy moments but nothing more than
you'd get on a typical British soap opera these days.
Buy this and a prepare to have some proper belly
laughs, I rarely laugh out loud to books but this one
makes you shake with mirth. Lee Sylvester.

****

DEAR COCA-COLA

Putting pen to paper with hilarious results, in Dear
Coca-Cola Terry Ravenscroft homes in on the Food &
Drink industry. Household names such as Heinz,
Ryvita, Tesco, Cadburys and of course the Coca-Cola
Company are the targets for his entertaining epistles,
resulting in a laugh-out-loud letters book with a
difference. And you don't want to know what he asks
Jacob's Biscuits for! But you will when you've read his
letters to them. You will never look at the contents of
your fridge or kitchen cupboards in the same way again.

Reader's review:- *I loved reading through this book of
funny letters. It's amazing how long Terry will keep up
the communication, but as long as the guy's answering
the letters keep doing just that, so will Terry and it just
so happens that he gets more and more ridiculous as
the replies get further in. I'd recommend this to anyone.*
Pete S.

****

LES DAWSON'S CISSIE AND ADA

The TV scripts written by scriptwriter Terry Ravenscroft for Les Dawson's famous Cissie & Ada characters. (Available as ebook only)

Reader's review:- *It was as I expected, superb! Terry over the years wrote some of the finest comedy seen on television, and the book was exactly as promised and the same as I'd expected.* Don Read.

****

I'M IN HEAVEN

I'm in Heaven is about a man who doesn't believe in God who dies and goes to heaven. However the heaven depicted in I'm in Heaven is far from being most people's vision of heaven - all sweetness and light and lazing about on a white cloud with angels playing harps - but something far, far different. Oh, and the Beatles are there. All of them, not just John and George. And Sir Michael Caine too. And Robert de Niro. And Jehovah's Witnesses don't like it at all.

Reader's review:- *Such an enjoyable read considering the very edgy subject matter; Religion, cancer and death. I loved it and read it in one go! Very thought provoking.* TC.

FOOTBALL CRAZY

If meat pie millionaire Joe Price had never bought lowly Coca-Cola League Two side Frogley Town and vowed to take them all the way to the top of the Premiership, if football fanatic Stanley Sutton hadn't dyed his dog Fentonbottom in the club's colours, if team manager Big Donny Donnelly hadn't had the acquisition of a mistress as his main priority, if local radio presenter Dave Rave and Frogley Advertiser sports journalist Martin Sneed hadn't wanted to chase their dreams, if the inmates of the local lunatic asylum hadn't numbered themselves among Frogley Town's keenest supporters and if Frogley police chief Superintendent Screwer hadn't sworn to rid the town of football hooligans, none of this would ever have happened. But unfortunately they all did. Football Crazy – a comic tale of football, sex, madness, sex, violence, and more sex.

Reader's review:- *One of the funniest books I've read in a long time. But don't read it on the train if you are embarrassed by laughing out loud. Satire at it's best - outrageous but with overtones of the truth.* Brian E Wotton.

****

THE RAZZAMATAZZ FUN EBOOK

The Razzamatazz Fun eBook is a collection of sketches, stories, parodies, humorous newspaper and magazine advertisements, quizzes, games, new book announcements, job applications, travel brochures, restaurant menus, cookbooks, theme park ads, wedding lists, you name it you'll probably find it inside. Plus an extensive comic encyclopaedia. (Available as ebook only)

Reader's review:- *If my parents had caught me reading this 45 years ago they would have wondered what on earth I was reading. If I had caught any of my children in their early teens reading it I would probably not have given them my approval! I'm a sad old ***t. I read this in just under two days. My wife does not share my humour. So I gave up trying to retell some of the contents. The day in the life of a cat!!!!! might just spare the life of our neighbours cat the next time she uses our seed bed as a litter tray. In the words of Oliver Twist ' Please Sir, can I have some more?' Read this on a bus and the men in white coats might just be waiting for you as you get off.* Anthony V.

****

ZEPHYR ZODIAC

Zephyr Zodiac is the story of a Mark 3 Ford Zephyr
Zodiac from the time it rolled off the production line in
1962 until it meets its end in a car crusher in 2012, and
how it affects the lives of seven of the people who own
it during that period. Read how during its fifty years on
this earth it was used as a company car, a family car, a
wedding car, a funeral car, a taxi, a home, a safe, a
Classic Car, how it was given birth in, stolen (more
than once), used to have sex in (much more than once),
and was instrumental in giving its grateful owner his
life back.

Reader's review:- *I have read several of Terry
Ravenscroft's books and they have all made me laugh,
but Zephyr Zodiac made me cry as well. I defy anyone
to get to the end of two of the stories, 'Walking Back To
Happiness' and 'Contented' without getting a big lump
in their throat. But they're still funny! Another must buy
from a writer who is fast becoming my favourite author.*
Mrs K Chesworth.

****

CALL ME A TAXI

Gary Allsop, a big Laurel & Hardy fan, is out of work,
has a spendthrift wife and a bleak future - and then he
meets Jim Moore, an even bigger Laurel & Hardy fan.

Call me a Taxi is a 22,500 word novella. (Available as ebook only)

Reader's review:- *I really enjoyed this book. Unlike so many books it has a beginning, a middle and ending - and a very satisfying, and apposite ending at that. I look forward to reading more of this author's work.* Daisy.

****

GOOD OLD GEORGE

A bleak future faces recently-demobbed World War Two soldiers Colin Arnfield and Ray Watson on their return to the depressing north west town of Milltown, until fate takes a hand.... Good Old George! is a 23,000 word novella. (Available as ebook only)

Reader's review:- *Super bit of writing from Mr.Ravenscroft,giving a joyous and sometimes poignant look at the post war class system.Never too preachy but often thought provoking.*
Keep 'em coming. Anthony Jennison.

****

STAIRLIFT TO HEAVEN 2 -
FURTHER UP THE STAIRLIFT

A further volume chronicling the life of an old age pensioner. There are more valuable lessons to be learned here in coping with old age, in addition to advice on how to deal with troublesome dogs, dog walking, horses, faith healers, gipsies, solicitors, council officials, busybodies, and sundry other nuisances, plus useful tips on hoovering, letter writing, mounting a defence should you be taken to court, coping with being sentenced to Community Service (if your defence in court has proved to be inadequate), how to get the best of, and avoid the worst of, a holiday in Turkey, what to do should your home be burgled, what to do if your bank has 'good news' for you and lots, lots more.

Reader's review:- *Can it be true? I split my sides laughing at Stairlift to Heaven but this sequel is even funnier! Great to be able to laugh again! A real recession antidote! Buy it!* Martin K Davies.

****

IT'S NOT CRICKET!

When the great ex-England cricket captain Jonny Pickering retires from the professional arena and comes to live in the village of Upper Medlock it is the most wonderful news the local cricket team have ever had. For with Jonny in their side victory will be theirs for the taking in the annual blood match against their bitter rivals Lower Medlock. But for some reason the Lower Medlock team believe they have as much right as Upper Medlock to Jonny Pickering's services. Pickering in the meantime is looking forward to a long and peaceful retirement. Some hopes!

Reader's review:- *Yet another great book from a writer who deserves far more fame than he has. All his books have a rich compendium of characters and this is no exception.* NigelGG

Lightning Source UK Ltd.
Milton Keynes UK
UKOW02f0758210515

252012UK00001B/9/P